"Avis Glaze's views on leadership are unique and powerful for one main reason. She puts things together that people don't usually think are compatible, thereby reaching new heights and depths of insight and efficacy. She combines empathy and determination; respect and candor; high expectations and persistent patience. The bottom line is as close to 100% success as possible, with every percentage point below 100 unacceptable. Accordingly, *Reaching the Heart of Leadership* is chock full of unusual insights. For each chapter there are lessons learned, and action steps to be taken, but understand that none of this is about slogans, and all of it has been tested and learned through hard practice. Avis does wear her heart on her sleeve; but also she wears it in every action relationship she encounters. For Avis, every value is a competency and every competency is a value. Read this book and be inspired to be the best leader you can ever be."

—**Michael Fullan, Professor Emeritus**
OISE/University of Toronto
Ontario, Canada

"If we truly want leaders who can foster supportive and inclusive school climates that focus on learning, we should start by having them reflect on their moral compass. In *Reaching the Heart of Leadership: Lessons Learned, Insights Gained, Actions Taken*, Avis Glaze leans on her deeply rich experience and offers, not only a call for moral purpose, but actions at each level to get leaders there. It is a wonderfully insightful and important read."

—**Peter DeWitt, EdD, Author/Consultant**
Finding Common Ground (Education Week)
Albany, NY

"Glaze's *Reaching the Heart of Leadership* speaks to an array of leaders—principals, teachers, community partners, families, and students, who, she insists, are at the epicenter of educational leadership. This book provides solid rationales, guidance and concrete actions on how educators can achieve and rise above the cacophony of demands for improved outcomes, higher standards, and increased accountability. Educators are encouraged to draw upon the competencies of empathy, advocacy, a strong human rights and social justice orientation, and a commitment to further action – with a sense of urgency. Glaze outlines an education that enhances students' critical and analytic stances on the world around them; develops their identities as empathetic local and global citizens; and animates and strengthens their multicultural, multilingual, and multi-literacy competencies in all curricular areas to deepen and broaden their learning and aspirations for their futures. This is an essential book for current and aspiring teachers and administrators."

—Allison Skerrett, PhD, Associate Professor
The University of Texas at Austin
Austin, TX

"Reaching the Heart of Leadership strikes a chord with each of us as it is practical, clear and concise. Dr. Avis Glaze speaks from experience, expertise and her heart in this succinct, action-guide for leaders at every level. Truly a must-read for all aspiring, inquiring educational leaders who want to make a difference for every learner in their care."

—Dr. Lyn Sharratt, International Education
Consultant and Author
OISE, University of Toronto
Ontario, Canada

"Dr. Avis Glaze shares the deep wisdom gained from her celebrated career in education. In *Reaching the Heart of Leadership*, she reflects on 'what she knows for sure' about the human condition and school leadership, and she reminds us all of the importance of putting people first, practicing empathy and developing positive relationships as the tools to impact school improvement. A master teacher always leaves us learning and reflecting. In this book, Dr. Glaze does just that. It's a 'must have' for your professional library."

—**Deirdre Kinsella Bliss, Editor,** *Principal*
Connections **Magazine**
Catholic Principals' Council
Ontario, Canada

"Reaching the Heart of Leadership deftly weaves together history, reflection, insights gained from lived experience, practical advice and inspiration. The mantra of 'leading from the heart" is both timely and timeless. Transcending education and educational leadership, the values espoused in this book easily extend across jurisdictions and to other scenarios that involve relationships of power."

—**Claudette Williams, PhD, Professor Emerita**
University of the West Indies, Jamaica
West Indies, Jamaica

Reaching the
Heart of Leadership

Corwin Impact Leadership Series

Series Editor: Peter M. DeWitt

Reaching the Heart of Leadership

Lessons Learned, Insights Gained, Actions Taken

Avis Glaze

A Joint Publication

A SAGE Publishing Company

FOR INFORMATION:

Corwin

A SAGE Company

2455 Teller Road

Thousand Oaks, California 91320

(800) 233-9936

www.corwin.com

SAGE Publications Ltd.

1 Oliver's Yard

55 City Road

London EC1Y 1SP

United Kingdom

SAGE Publications India Pvt. Ltd.

B 1/I 1 Mohan Cooperative Industrial Area

Mathura Road, New Delhi 110 044

India

SAGE Publications Asia-Pacific Pte. Ltd.

3 Church Street

#10-04 Samsung Hub

Singapore 049483

Printed in the United States of America

Names: Glaze, Avis, author.

Title: Reaching the heart of leadership : lessons learned, insights gained, actions taken / Avis E. Glaze.

Description: Thousand Oaks : Corwin, [2017] | Includes bibliographical references and index.

Identifiers: LCCN 2017012439 | ISBN 9781506325323 (pbk. : acid-free paper)

Subjects: LCSH: Educational leadership. | Educational leadership—Moral and ethical aspects. | Motivation in education.

Classification: LCC LB2806 .G53 2017 | DDC 371.2—dc23

LC record available at https://lccn.loc.gov/2017012439

This book is printed on acid-free paper.

Executive Editor: Arnis Burvikovs

Senior Associate Editor: Desirée A. Bartlett

Editorial Assistant: Kaitlyn Irwin

Production Editor: Amy Schroller

Copy Editor: Laureen Gleason

Typesetter: C&M Digitals (P) Ltd.

Proofreader: Dennis W. Webb

Indexer: Amy Murphy

Cover Designer: Michael Dubowe

Marketing Manager: Nicole Franks

Certified Chain of Custody
SUSTAINABLE   Promoting Sustainable Forestry
FORESTRY   www.sfiprogram.org
INITIATIVE   SFI-01268
SFI label applies to text stock

17 18 19 20 21 10 9 8 7 6 5 4 3 2 1

Contents

Preface

Educators are certainly making significant strides in their efforts to educate more children successfully. Graduation rates have been increasing steadily in many jurisdictions, and dropout rates are decreasing. The focus on effective teaching has become a characteristic of most systems that have a strong commitment to continuous improvement.

At critical intervals in our evolution as mature organizations, it is essential that we take time to acknowledge our efforts, identify our successes, determine what remains to be done, and direct our energies toward reaching new heights of leadership effectiveness.

This short book is about the wise application of power and influence and the need to accentuate and strengthen the bonds of trust that we must forge as leaders. It identifies the need to avoid certainty and, instead, to ignite the intellectual curiosity and "other-directedness" that is needed to prepare students to be global citizens in an increasingly interdependent world—students who think critically, analytically, and strategically; who feel deeply and empathically; and who act wisely, decisively, and ethically.

Acknowledgments

As leaders reflect on their careers, there are always recurring themes that emerge. They relate to the leaders' educational philosophy, beliefs about human nature, leadership style, results achieved, and impact on the people and organizations they had the privilege of influencing. It is often their personal mission to leave a legacy that clearly demonstrates that their actions aligned with the values and beliefs that they espoused. Leaders in general, and educational leaders in particular, hope that people who have worked with them can say, "Yes, those are, indeed, the beliefs, guiding principles, and behaviors that they demonstrated." In other words, "That's exactly how they behaved."

One can only hope that one's professional imperative has been to bring about meaningful change where needed—changes that have an enduring impact on people and their organizational culture by reaching the heart of leadership. This means, among other things, cultures that are healthy, people- and results-oriented, focused on capacity building, and responsive to change. It also means becoming instruments of change and reflective stewards, constantly honing our skills and cogitating the reasons we chose leadership in the first place.

It is with heartfelt gratitude that I recognize a few individuals who, through their examples, have reinforced my philosophy in the potential of leadership to realize the outcomes for which we have all fought. They have epitomized the leadership that we strive to emulate and the qualities that ignite curiosity, stir people to act, and, ultimately, reach the heart of leadership.

First, my sincere gratitude to Arnis Burvikovs, without whose instigation I would not have completed this book. He accommodated my changing timelines with reassurance and encouragement and demonstrated empathy—a quintessential leadership quality that is discussed in this book. Peter Dewitt and the outstanding team at Corwin deserve special acknowledgment for the support that they provided.

Bill Hogarth, former director of education at the York Region District School Board, and Ruth Mattingley, former superintendent of schools and senior executive officer of the Literacy and Numeracy Secretariat, with whom I worked, always serve as models of what effective leadership looks like. I depend on them to challenge my thinking and insights. Their leadership philosophy, values, and modus operandi consistently reflect the importance of reaching the heart in leadership.

There are also the graduate students at the Ontario Institute for Studies in Education with whom I have worked. I am reassured that these young academics, many of whom will be working in education, will continue the research-into-practice orientation that will help improve our education systems. Crystal Bender deserves special recognition for her editorial and research assistance regarding the references in this book.

Michael Fullan has had a strong influence on us over the years. One of the things I have always admired about his writing is that he recognizes the role of affect in teaching, learning, and leadership. He knows that we do not get things done simply by issuing edicts, rules, and regulations. For Michael, leaders must be guided by a moral imperative and the skills to inspire people to act.

My thanks to Peter Bailey, my husband, whom I can always call on to give me feedback on my ideas. He is my toughest "critical friend"—one who never wants to be thanked—especially in this way. But I cannot ignore his contribution, because of his constant advice: "Just get it done!"

I will always be grateful to the many individuals with whom I have worked across the globe, during my early years as an educator in

Jamaica, during my career at Ontario's Literacy and Numeracy Secretariat, and in the York Region and Kawartha Pine Ridge District School Boards. They have all been a source of inspiration and have left an indelible stamp in their inimitable ways. Their influence and their reach have no limits.

About the Author

Avis Glaze is an international leader in the field of education. As one of Canada's outstanding educators, she has been recognized for her work in leadership development, student achievement, school and system improvement, character development, and equity of outcomes for all students. As Ontario's first chief student achievement officer and founding CEO of the Literacy and Numeracy Secretariat, she played a pivotal role in improving student achievement in Ontario schools. Her primary focus in education is on building capacity to ensure that all students achieve, regardless of background factors or personal circumstances. It is her core belief that educators play a fundamental role in sustaining democracy.

Dr. Glaze completed two Master of Education programs—one in educational administration and a second in guidance and counseling—and a Doctorate in Education at the Ontario Institute for Studies in Education, University of Toronto. She also has training in alternative dispute resolution, advanced facilitation, and the assessment of emotional intelligence. She has taught at all levels of the education system, in rural and urban areas, in public and Catholic schools, and at the elementary, secondary, community college, and university levels. Dr. Glaze has been a superintendent of schools in several school districts, an associate director of education with the York Region District School Board, and director of education of the Kawartha Pine Ridge District School Board. At the university level, Dr. Glaze has been an adjunct professor in counselor and teacher education in faculties of education in Ontario. She also served as an education officer with the Ontario Ministry of Education and as a research coordinator with the Ontario Women's Directorate of the Ministry of Labour.

In 1994, Dr. Glaze served as a commissioner on the Ontario Royal Commission on Learning and had the opportunity to influence the direction of education in Ontario through the recommendations of the commission. She has extensive experience in international education and was chosen by the Canadian government to assist with educational reform in South Africa. She represented Canada at the UNESCO conference on inclusive education in Riga, Latvia. In addition, she knows schools across the globe firsthand, having worked with educators in Australia, England, Finland, Singapore, Ireland, Scotland, Germany, the Caribbean, and many parts of the United States.

Within her community, she served as chairperson of the Harry R. Gairey Scholarship Fund, helping outstanding black students attend university. She established the Avis Glaze Scholarships with the Markham African Caribbean Association for university or college education and has supported a scholarship for studies in education at the University of Ottawa.

Dr. Glaze has received honorary doctorates from several Canadian universities and has won more than forty awards for outstanding contribution to education, including Educator of the Year, the Distinguished Educator Award, the 2001 YWCA Women of Distinction Award, the Harry Jerome Award, the Sandford D. McDonnell Lifetime Achievement Award for Character Education offered by the Character Education Partnership in the United States, and the Order of Ontario, among others. Most recently, she was honored by The Learning Partnership for her contribution to public education.

After serving as Ontario's first CEO of the Literacy and Numeracy Secretariat, Dr. Glaze was later appointed as Ontario's education commissioner and senior adviser to the minister of education. Her consulting company, Edu-quest International Inc., offers a wide range of services internationally. She continues to motivate and inspire educators through speaking engagements and consults with school districts, nonprofit organizations, and businesses to maximize talent and achieve results. She assisted with education reform in South Africa and later served as adviser on national standards to the minister of education in New Zealand. Dr. Glaze continues to be the inveterate learner that she is, taking courses at every possible opportunity. She recently received designation as a Visible Learning certified trainer in John Hattie's work, offered through Corwin in Thousand Oaks, California.

Dr. Glaze is a consummate capacity builder in teaching, improving student achievement, leadership development, and school system improvement. She is skilled at motivating and inspiring teachers, principals, system leaders, policymakers, politicians, parents, and business leaders to realize their potential in improving their schools. She coauthored *Breaking Barriers: Excellence and Equity for All* (Glaze, Mattingley, & Levin, 2012) on the high-impact strategies to improve education systems in general, and schools in particular. Her most recent book, *High School Graduation: K–12 Strategies That Work* (Glaze, Mattingley, & Andrews, 2013), identifies the research-informed strategies to improve graduation rates for all students, regardless of socioeconomic or other social or demographic factors.

Dr. Glaze's international contributions were once again recognized when she received the Robert Owen Award, the first of its kind offered in Scotland. She was also invited to Norway by Queen Sonya to address the issue of how schools can build better societies. Most recently, she was appointed as one of the international education advisers to help overhaul the Scottish education system, focusing on the government priorities of closing the attainment gap, achieving equity, and system reform.

Please visit her website at www.avisglaze.ca.

1

Reaching the Heart of Leadership

The heart is a muscle, and you strengthen muscles by using them.
The more I lead with my heart, the stronger it gets.

(Miller, 2013)

Metaphorically, the heart represents the central organ of the human body and is seen as a major source of emotions, humane feelings, and positive personal attributes. It exemplifies sincerity, bravery, audacity, and zeal. It represents the core. Indeed, in many cultures and religions, the heart symbolizes moral courage—a theme that runs throughout this book.

Leaders want to be successful in their roles. Organizations are investing heavily in leadership development in order to foster the qualities that make a difference. They are fully aware of those qualities that are a recipe for failure. This includes leaders who are heartless and lacking in courage, kindness, enthusiasm, generosity, or magnanimity. If organizations are to be effective, and if we are to build public confidence in our institutions, individuals exhibiting these deficits must be excluded from or counseled out of leadership roles.

The heart of leadership is about reaching the core and tapping into what moves and motivates people toward the achievement of goals that make a difference in people's lives. It is grounded in a leader's courageous and unwavering commitment to doing what's right and to being motivated by a moral imperative. It is about taking seriously the needs and aspirations of people who do the work required each day for the organization to succeed.

In education, it is about ensuring the centrality of the needs of the student, as the learner, in all decisions. It is about ensuring that every student succeeds, regardless of his or her race, gender, socio-economic status, or other personal characteristics or life circum-stances. It is about disaggregating the data to ensure that students receive appropriate interventions and supports. It is about paying assiduous attention to the needs of individual students and the groups to which they belong.

In education, being a strong advocate for students is at the heart of effective leadership. Ensuring that the workplace is devoid of fear and that teachers and principals are supported to do their best work is another essential component. Making sure that parents and the public have a voice in determining the goals and effective-ness of the system counts as well.

When one reaches the heart of leadership, one assumes a new level of stewardship. And that stewardship requires an intense focus on capacity building in order to bring about the changes and to achieve the outcomes that are necessary for new energy, enthusiasm, and vitality to thrive. Reaching the heart unleashes the entrepreneurial spirit and innovative thinking that enables creative decision making to permeate all aspects and levels of the organization.

Reaching the heart is about enhancing life chances and achieving results for students who have not succeeded historically and who have not yet realized their potential, either as individuals or as members of the groups to which they belong. To use the commonly cited phrase, it is about raising the bar for all students and closing achievement gaps between groups. It is about talking courageous stances—never succumbing to paralysis or inaction but, instead, being blatantly opportunistic in addressing students' needs. As leaders, we must continue to ignite students' intellectual curiosity and encourage an inclusive worldview. For these students, reaching the heart of leadership means that they must become the solution finders who are willing to address issues such as indifference, neutrality, or injustice, wherever they exist.

As educational leaders, one of the privileges of professionalism is that we are entrusted with the lives of students and the responsibility of improving work environments and learning cultures. It is about having high expectations for ourselves, students, and staff; developing a strong commitment to research-informed strategies, holistic approaches, and fidelity to what works; and also influencing educational systems and holding them in trust for future generations. Most important, it is about the ability to demonstrate moral outrage when commonly held universal values are infringed upon.

- - - - - Leadership Lessons Learned

Over the years, I have learned that it is necessary to

1. Work assiduously at becoming a truly reflective leader—one who is increasingly aware of and demonstrates respect for the needs of the people we serve.

2. Acknowledge that all people have biases and prejudices that have surreptitiously crept into their consciousness over the years. What is important is a willingness to work to address those biases.

3. Demonstrate empathy for employees, whenever possible, and have a strong commitment to address their needs in the workplace.

4. Recognize that "whenever there is unequal distribution of power, the relationship becomes a moral one," (Sergiovanni, 2001) and adhere to a moral imperative in the way we treat those we lead.

5. Think critically about the decisions we make in terms of our own motivations and intentions, but, more important, in terms of the impact they have on others.

● ● ● ● ACTION STEPS FOR REACHING THE HEART OF LEADERSHIP

To reach the heart, it is necessary to

1. Seek every opportunity to read alternative perspectives that will elucidate issues related to how we use power and privilege.

2. Access programs related to sensitivity training, antiracism, and the prohibited grounds covered by human rights codes—for example, regarding avoiding discrimination based on race, gender, and religion, among others.

3. Ensure that issues such as poverty do not determine destiny, recognizing that socioeconomic biases, though not a part of these codes, are a very important consideration in education.

4. Through deep reflection and training, work at dislodging any prejudices or biases that we may have absorbed over the years and learn how to become more effective in working with people from diverse groups.

5. Identify formally and informally a few trusted employees at different levels of the organization—for example, a secretary, custodian, parent, or student leader—and empower them to give you feedback on how you use position power and on your behaviors and attitudes that may be inconsistent with what you preach or the values of the organization.

6. Work collaboratively with a team to establish norms of reflective practice, ensuring that open, honest, and direct feedback is an expectation.

7. Seek every opportunity to gather information on, talk about, and improve the interpersonal dynamics within your organization.

8. Provide human relations and interpersonal skills development, as well as assertiveness training, at all levels of your system. Include student leaders in these initiatives.

9. Create a culture devoid of a fear of reprisals in which everyone, regardless of where they are on the organization ladder, has the responsibility to point out to others when they are not being respectful.

10. Disseminate questionnaires with specific questions about your leadership style, attitudes, behaviors, and interpersonal competences. These should be anonymous and sent to a trusted employee identified beforehand, whose role is to summarize these comments and present the summary to the leader, who should share the findings unaltered in an honest and nondefensive manner with colleagues. This process should include a plan on how these comments will be addressed.

11. Encourage staff to do the same feedback exercise with their students. This exercise will be helpful only if it is conducted in a climate of trust and congeniality.

12. In Chapter 2, we will review Kovach's (1987) research on what motivates employees. Following this model, work with employees to identify the relationship and culture-related variables that are important in your organization. Ask employees to rank these variables in order of importance and ask senior administrators to rank them as well. Discuss the rankings; try to arrive at a consensus of what is needed to take your organization to new levels of performance effectiveness. Devise a plan of action for improvement.

2

Leadership Then . . . and Now

REFLECTIONS ON LEADERSHIP

It is truly exhilarating to be at a stage at which one has time to reflect on one's career and to identify the takeaways from the time spent in progressively responsible leadership roles along the way. To reach the heart of leadership, one needs to engage in deep reflection and to ask oneself some soul-searching questions at each stage along one's leadership trajectory, rather than waiting until the end of one's career. By doing this systematically, one has the opportunity to reflect, take stock, devise a plan, formulate corrective actions, and make improvements, as required. These questions for reflection should include the following:

Questions for Self-Analysis and Reflection

- What are the reasons I chose to seek out progressively responsible leadership positions?

- Was I propelled by causes outside of myself, or was I motivated by self-interest?

- Was I as magnanimous as I could possibly have been along the way?

- Did I listen to my inner radar and follow my inner compass?

- Was I bound by moral and ethical imperatives?

- Did I practice what I preached?

- Did I address the major sources of ambivalence and surprise?

- Did I pay attention to the opinions, needs, and aspirations of those expected to do the daily work?

- Did my organization and the morale of employees thrive under my leadership?

- Did I communicate widely and work with the widest possible cross-section of people to embed key leadership beliefs, values, goals, and expectations into the fabric of the organization?

- Did I co-opt, train, and support future leaders with the skills required to sustain and build upon the gains?

At critical points in one's career, there is a need to engage in introspection and reflection—a soul-searching borne out of a desire for assurance that there was congruence among knowledge, beliefs, values, motivations, and behaviors. The need for a convergence of values and behaviors is a leadership imperative that unearths all that one has stood for and fought for over the years. This exercise also highlights the practices that can be discarded and elucidates the ones that must be kept alive. And for those who spend their lives in search of truth, genuineness, and fidelity to longstanding universal values, the answers can make a difference in the way one assesses the success of one's career.

The insights gained from this exercise will also affect the sense of contentment that one hopes to achieve in retirement, when one inevitably will have time to look back and think deeply about one's actions and achievements. It also influences the ability to arrive at a conclusion as to whether or not one has fought a good fight, achieved the desired outcomes, and demonstrated the character and personal attributes that a leader could only hope would be his or her leadership legacy.

Leaders today must have a strong determination to ensure that they contribute to their sense of satisfaction that they did, indeed, work hard to demonstrate the personal attributes they say they value most. These include integrity, empathy, courage, optimism, and respect.

Among these attributes, demonstrating respect is the most fundamental and all-encompassing if one wants to reach the heart of leadership. Based on what we know about the qualities that have a lasting impact on organizational cultures and on people's lives, respect should include respect for self, others, cultural differences, diversity, and human rights, to name a few. These are fundamental to and form the basis of healthy, effective, and productive relationships in any setting—be it the home, the workplace, or the community—and with all individuals—our children, relatives, friends, or professional colleagues. More than ever, leaders today require a deeply held conviction that respect is the *sine qua non* in effective interpersonal relationships.

The way we treat people along our leadership journey can eventually enhance or hinder our career progression and upward mobility. Examples abound of leaders who failed because they did not demonstrate these interpersonal competencies. Moreover, people do not easily forget how they were treated; when they are treated poorly, it remains with them and affects them for a long time.

In some jurisdictions, before anyone is promoted to a leadership role, those who will eventually make the decision conduct site visits and hold interviews with individuals with whom the aspiring candidate worked in earlier positions. The questions asked at these site visits are geared toward unearthing the behaviors the aspirant demonstrated in those settings. Respect for others, especially those at the lower rungs of the organizational hierarchy, is always included in this probing exercise. Why? Because demonstrating respect for others is a competence that is at the heart of leadership.

I remember quite vividly an example of a situation where key community members believed that a principal did not show respect for her community in terms of their values, their beliefs, and their expectations of the school. I had to intervene after giving the principal ample support and leeway to put the relationship back on track. Eventually, the principal had no choice but to resign. Trust, once lost, is almost impossible to regain. It takes inordinate effort to redress such situations. This all started with what the community described as a lack of recognition and respect for their deeply held values and a principal who, they felt, was either unwilling or unable to turn the situation around.

Admittedly, there are times when a leader must challenge the values of a community if these values are inhumane or inconsistent with organization values. If one encounters a situation, for example, in which there are deep-seated biases and prejudices, unfair behavior, or disrespect shown toward individuals and groups, a leader must take a stand, responding quickly and decisively. But any leader who chooses to take on the community or other groups of individuals must recognize the strength, stamina, and support from one's supervisors and colleagues that is required when one becomes embroiled in such conflicts.

Nonetheless, in all such situations one must always be guided by a strong sense of moral imperative and the need to act according to one's conscience.

Martin Luther King Jr. provides some insights on this theme. He once said,

> On some positions, cowardice asks the question, is it expedient? And then expedience comes along and asks the question,

is it politic? Vanity asks the question, is it popular? Conscience asks the question, is it right? There comes a time when one must take the position that is neither safe nor politic nor popular, but he must do it because conscience tells him it is right.

This civil rights icon was alluding to our modern notion of moral imperative. Many educators today use this term regularly to describe their motivation in making decisions in schools. Often, we use this to test actions related to the life chances of students and their role in ensuring that their actions can withstand the highest test—is this the right course of action in this situation?

Deep introspection helps leaders reflect on the leadership lessons learned and insights gained over time. Because these lessons represent the seeds they have sown and determine the reputation that remains throughout their career and lifetime, it is important for leaders to think deeply about the impact they are having on the people they serve, their colleagues, and the organizations they lead.

When I was a secondary school vice principal, I had very high expectations of staff—similar to those I had for myself. My main motivation was to get things done quickly for the benefit of students. My popular refrain was "the children cannot wait." I felt that their time in school was finite and that we should not waste it in any way. Things had to be done with a sense of urgency in order to achieve the outcomes that we had established for the students. In that situation, what I wanted was to have all staff members involved with students outside of their regular teaching duties. This meant that teachers were being asked to assume some form of extracurricular activities to support student engagement and well-being.

One of the oldest members of the staff—someone close to retirement— came to my office to see me. He told me that he couldn't do any more than he was currently doing because his wife was very ill and he was having serious problems with his teenage son. I was so touched with his sincerity and pain that I began to cry. I remember vividly my reflections at the moment. I thought to myself,

Here you are, thinking you are a cracker-jack vice principal, always talking about how important empathy is, how empathetic you are, and how much you care about people. But you were not being considerate of the needs of all your staff members in this case! You were more interested in getting things done than considering the needs of the people who are expected to do the work.

Through deep introspection, I decided that it was necessary to change my behavior in a manner that was more consistent with the values I espoused and openly expressed on many occasions. In other words, I knew I had to work harder at practicing what I was preaching. This incident was a catalyst in my career—a watershed moment. I became more self-aware and more vigilant, and monitored more closely how I behaved toward the people I supervised. It was a life lesson learned that stayed with me throughout my career as a leader. This incident and the accompanying takeaways also had implications for relationships in other contexts.

I once again reflected on Tom Sergiovanni's notion of the morality inherent in relationships when there is unequal distribution of power, articulated in his book *Value-Added Leadership* (1990). As a young administrator, I took this very seriously. In fact, this became a mantra throughout the years I spent in educational leadership. Within the organizations in which I worked, I recognized the "power" and the responsibility that accompanied the positions I had. I also sought out the rich body of research that exists in the educational literature on the topic of "position power."

Having position power means that it is incumbent upon leaders to use the power that accompanies leadership roles wisely and ethically. How a leader treats the custodians, the secretaries, the clerks in the finance department, or the mom or dad from the poorest part of the community matters significantly! It is so easy for leaders to treat people differentially in terms of the respect and attention shown to them, based on a host of factors if leaders do not have the values-driven, people-oriented inner radar that helps monitor their behavior. Biases and prejudices that we have all picked up along the way can surreptitiously undermine our best intentions. They can greatly influence the behavior of even those leaders who consider themselves to be fair-minded individuals who have acknowledged, and continue to work on, dislodging their own biases and prejudices.

Self-knowledge and awareness are enhanced when leaders take the time to think critically about their role, decisions, intentions, motivations, and *modus operandi*. Most important, it would serve leaders well to think long and hard about the meaning of power, privilege, and entitlement in their own lives and how they use this when they are entrusted with positions of added responsibility. This awareness, when acted upon, can be a source for either leadership success or dismal failure in the role when it is underdeveloped.

On the question of how leaders use power, which was mentioned earlier, it is important for leaders to reject the "power over" mentality in their pronouncements about who they are when describing their leadership style. Over the years, I have seen the impact that this type of leadership has had and the havoc it has inflicted on people's lives, sense of well-being, and job satisfaction. On the other hand, when leaders understand themselves and what having real power means, they eschew negative notions of power and adopt more positive approaches. They see power as working with and through people to get things done and to realize their goals. They take seriously how they lead and reflect on issues such as what it takes to motivate and inspire people so that they can realize their full potential and contribute to the collective success.

On the question of what motivates people, there are many lessons to be learned from the work of Kovach (1987), who asked employers and employees to rank order some key variables to answer the question "What motivates employees?" What is most instructive is the difference between the responses:

What Motivates Employees?	
Employers' Response	*Employees' Response*
1. Dollars	1. Appreciation
2. Job security	2. Feeling of belonging
3. Promotions	3. Sympathy for personal problems
4. Working conditions	4. Interesting work

(Continued)

(Continued)

Employers' Response	Employees' Response
5. Interesting work	5. Job security
6. Loyalty from company	6. Dollars
7. Tactful disciplining	7. Promotions
8. Appreciation	8. Loyalty from company
9. Sympathy for personal problems	9. Working conditions
10. Feeling of belonging	10. Tactful disciplining

The top three variables for employers—dollars, job security, and promotions—are consistent with the perspectives of some of today's leaders in relation to their employees. It is worth comparing these with the top three variables chosen by employees—namely, appreciation, a feeling of belonging, and sympathy for personal problems.

WHAT MOTIVATES EMPLOYEES THE MOST?

Appreciation

When I was a superintendent of schools, many principals shared their feelings with me from time to time on how much they valued being told that their work was appreciated and that a supervisor valued qualities such as their commitment to students and work ethic. Direct, specific, meaningful, and genuine feedback motivated them to do even more and to be better at what they did. Their comments included popular sayings such as "You can catch bees with honey—not vinegar!" These were confident, successful adults! One could be so easily tempted to think that they did not need to be affirmed and validated. But another lesson that we can all learn is that even the most confident and successful employees thrive on being validated by their supervisors. There is almost a human need for reaffirmation—especially from those who have the responsibility to evaluate performance or to determine one's promotion.

Feeling of Belonging

The second on this list—a feeling of belonging—should not be underestimated, either. A workplace that has this ethos is also one that has lower turnover rates. People want to be there. There is a sense of collegiality—a notion that goes beyond congeniality. Sergiovanni (1990) used these terms and made distinctions between them years ago. More recently, others, such as Jasper (2014), have made similar observations. Where true collegiality exists, people are highly motivated to work toward common goals and outcomes.

Kathleen Jasper (2014) also makes a distinction between congeniality and collegiality and highlighted the effects of these qualities on organizations as follows:

> *Congenial* is [being] friendly, good-natured and hospitable. Congeniality is a decent attribute for an organization to have—people are nice to each other and staff is compliant. However, a good-natured, compliant staff does not necessarily yield increased creativity or productivity. In addition, friendly, congenial systems are sometimes a façade distinguishing a hierarchal structure where most of the decisions are made using a top-down approach. . . .
>
> *Collegial* on the other hand means shared, mutual and inter-related; decisions are made together and responsibility is communal. It's more than being friendly; it's getting work done in an effective way as a team by identifying opportunities for improvement and solving problems together. Collegiality is often a catalyst for difficult conversations, contention and even conflict to take place. Ultimately, collegiality is essential for impactful work to transpire.

More recent work on professional learning communities (PLCs) has highlighted the difference between congeniality and collegiality. My own observation is that the change in behaviors of those engaged in PLCs over the years has been phenomenal. In the early years, when there wasn't a deep understanding of how PLCs operate at their best, there were superficial notions of what successful PLCs looked like. People falsely equated "noise" with a real desire to solve problems related to the school. Consequently, they did not ensure that improvement was the primary reason for these gatherings. There has, however, been a discernible difference in how PLCs are functioning today. Educators have expanded their ideas about PLCs with the research that has been available in recent years. As noted above, PLCs can have a real impact when collegiality is at its best.

Sympathy for Personal Problems

The third variable ranked by employees is "sympathy for personal problems." Employees do not leave their problems at home or at the front gate of the school. The issues that they are facing at home or in the community are always with them. Only a few individuals can simply shake off problems, do their jobs, and pick up later from where they left off the previous day. Their concerns on and off the job can affect their interactions with their colleagues and students.

I remember working with a principal who suggested to staff that they should leave their problems behind and not take them into his school. His unwillingness to see staff members in their multiple roles—as coaches, parents, religious leaders, or community members—reflected his lack of a strong people orientation in the workplace. Not surprisingly, he was neither liked nor respected. People would not go to him if they had personal problems.

Being attuned to the personal problems of staff can help aspiring and seasoned leaders alike see people in the totality of their human character, qualities, values, aspirations, and world views. It also helps them suspend judgment when problems or conflicts arise. Asking the custodian about her sick child, taking a first-period class for a teacher who had a dental appointment, or covering for the school secretary who is going through a divorce can make a difference in the culture of the school and the relationships that are forged. It is in small ways that we demonstrate our humanity, caring, and concern for others in the workplace. And instead of using the term "sympathy" for personal problems, I would make a slight change to take this idea to a new level by describing this variable as "empathy for personal problems."

EMPATHY: A QUINTESSENTIAL LEADERSHIP COMPETENCE

The ability to be empathetic has profound implications for the way we engage one another at an interpersonal level. It is the quintessential human characteristic—one that demonstrates genuineness and loyalty and engenders a strong sense of connection with people. *Empathy* describes the feeling or reaction that most people welcome, especially when they are having problems.

In his recent book, *The Formative Five: Fostering Grit, Empathy, and Other Success Skills Every Student Needs*, Thomas Hoerr (2017) discusses recent research on empathy and makes a persuasive case for the importance of empathy in human endeavors. He rightly makes a distinction between empathy and sympathy, stating that we can sympathize with the plights of others without fully understanding, appreciating, or empathizing with their unique perspectives.

He starts his discussion with empathy because, in his own words,

> As I have grown older, I have come to value its importance more and more. When I think about the qualities I want in work colleagues, I realize that kindness and care are at the top of the list. Of course, knowledge, skills and work ethic are incredibly important, but I spend a lot of time and invest a great deal of emotional energy at work, so I want to be able to trust and lean on the people around me. (Hoerr, 2017, p. 36)

Hoerr refers to the centrality of empathy in teaching, its importance as a business attribute, and the fact that there is enough of it to go around when we practice this skill. He emphasizes that relationships are destined to fail in its absence. He states that history has taught us that a mass lack of empathy can lead to mass cruelty and the tendency to divide people into "us" and "them," which can lead to suspicion, miscommunication, and conflict. Not surprisingly, he states that bullying, a problem being addressed in many school districts today because of its long-lasting consequences, results from a lack of empathy. He acknowledges that it is human nature to "retreat to our tribe and to feel most comfortable among those who look, act, and think like us" (Hoerr, 2017).

He also offers six basic steps and a few strategies for developing empathy, as we teach this skill to our students in the same way we approach teaching other skills. These steps include the following:

1. Listening
2. Understanding
3. Internalizing
4. Projecting
5. Planning
6. Intervening

● ● ● ● HOW TO TAKE ACTION FOR DEVELOPING EMPATHY

Hoer (2017) offers concrete actions to develop empathy.

For all teachers:

- Help students recognize and understand the perspectives of others.
- Help students engage in service learning.
- Help students appreciate their own backgrounds and biases.
- Create safe spaces for students to tell their stories.
- Consciously teach about stereotypes and discrimination, the history and evolution of attitudes, and the reasons why people's degrees of empathy toward different people vary.
- Help students examine historical examples of innocent people who were wrongly accused of crimes.
- Always encourage students to consider situations from a variety of perspectives.
- Assign books that feature a diversity of humanity.
- Create a system by which students can submit anonymous compliments for specific classmates.
- Get students involved in charitable causes.

For middle and high school teachers:

- Teach students about the differences in perspective between journalism and literature and between current and historical accounts.
- Involve speakers who can give "the story behind the headlines."
- Read portions of Paul Theroux's book *Deep South* (2015) with students to examine a slice of life with which they may not be familiar.
- Draw content from *Material World: A Global Family Portrait* (1995) by Peter Menzel and Charles Mann.

For elementary school teachers:

- Teach students the difference between sympathy and empathy.
- Use empathy as a tool to help students understand character creation and development in fiction.
- Use games and competitions to help students see situations from others' perspectives.
- Ask students to speculate as to what other children might like to receive for their birthdays—discounting what they might want for themselves.
- If a student's pet dies, use the occasion to talk about feelings.

For principals:

- Make it a priority to hire teachers who are empathetic toward all kinds of students—not just those who excel in school and are well-behaved.
- Work to help teachers appreciate their students' home and community environments.
- Sponsor special thematic events, such as "Empathy Night."
- Create a social action committee among faculty to help students (and possibly parents) make a difference in the community.
- Screen books on topics such as empathy for discussion with colleagues and students.
- Form a voluntary faculty book group to read books related to empathy.

As an educator, I cannot emphasize enough how careful one must be in selecting books for use in schools. It is not about censorship, as some will say. It is about ensuring that the same students do not have to spend their entire careers feeling that they, and the groups to which they belong, are never presented in a positive light. As a superintendent of schools, I have been called by students who are crying and asking if they have to remain in classes in which they are presented in a negative light. What is unfortunate is that these groups never have the opportunity to see themselves or their groups presented positively.

Teachers and principals are encouraged to make sure that students and their backgrounds are presented positively and that students have avenues to share their thoughts and feelings about the content of the curriculum and its impact on them. It is important to acknowledge that there is a serious problem when students and their backgrounds are consistently portrayed negatively in the books to which they are exposed in the classroom. If students and their cultures are never portrayed positively, there is a great imbalance in what they will take away. So many students from diverse backgrounds have complained over the years about the negative impact of how they are portrayed. It is important for teachers and school leaders to see this as an unfairness for students in general, and for students from minority backgrounds in particular. So often, when I expressed the complaints of many students and parents, the response was, "These are the classics!" My response was, "The classics for whom?"

I was very impressed with education in New Zealand when I served as adviser to the minister of education. One of the tenets of the curriculum at the time should serve as a lesson to all of us: *"The curriculum should not alienate the students."*

I hasten to admit that in recent years I have met many teachers and principals who are attuned to these issues and are making every effort to ensure that their schools are implementing equitable and inclusive education practices. In fact, in Ontario, for example, we have developed many documents to address this and other equity issues. Once such document is *Realizing the Promise of Diversity: Ontario's Equity and Inclusive Education Strategy* (2009), available at www.edu.gov.on.ca/eng/policyfunding/equity.pdf.

This award-winning document, which is being implemented in Ontario schools, was designed to make concrete suggestions and provide opportunities for all students to reach their fullest potential. The document acknowledges that publicly funded education is the cornerstone of democracy, preparing students for their role in society as engaged, productive, and responsible citizens. It recognizes that some groups of students, including recent immigrants, children from low-income families, aboriginal students, boys, and students with special education needs, among others, may be at risk of lower achievement if concerted efforts are not taken to address these issues. The document lays out a clear vision for equity and asserts that excellence and equity must go hand in hand. They are, by no means, diametrically opposed. Instead, they are two sides of the same coin at least, and often on the same continuum, at best. The document emphasizes the fact that an equitable and inclusive education system is fundamental in realizing high levels of student achievement and is central in creating a cohesive society and a strong economy to secure Ontario's future prosperity.

Framed within the context of the province's Human Rights Code, this strategy envisions an education system in which

- All students, parents, and other members of the school community are welcomed and respected.
- Every student is supported and inspired to succeed in a culture of high expectations for learning.

Early in my leadership career, I developed and taught a course for leaders. It was called "Human Relations in Education." I was motivated by the fact that the leaders whom I considered to be effective all possessed a constellation of skills that are now being described in business and other fields as "people skills" or interpersonal competencies. What was interesting at the time was that there was so much focus in principal training programs on emphasizing operational skills—budgets, timetabling, staffing, and plant operations, among others. Admittedly, every aspiring leader should have at least a baseline knowledge of operational functions. My contention is that these tasks were being emphasized at the exclusion of the skills that I felt, from experience, were required to be effective leaders of people and to transform organizations, among other important goals.

It was not surprising that some of the individuals who failed miserably as principals or superintendents or in business could perform operational duties very well. But their Achilles' heel was their inability to lead and work effectively with people.

My experience in education tells me that both skill sets are needed if organizations are to function effectively. The issue is that we should not hide behind the operational duties, because these are not the ones that take organizations to new levels of attainment. It is through people and capacity building that we are able to move organizations to the apex or pinnacle of performance and greater levels of achievement.

Teaching human relations and interpersonal competencies must become an essential component of leadership development programs.

LEADERSHIP: A BRIEF HISTORICAL OVERVIEW

When taken seriously, leadership does present its challenges. But those who aspire and prepare to assume leadership roles do recognize that it will not be easy. So, they fortify themselves to deal with the eventualities. For all leaders, this means not engaging in self-pity when times get rough. It doesn't take long to learn that it is important to be tough and resilient and to develop a thick skin. But that toughness in leadership should not be of the "muscle-flexing" kind. It has to be a principled toughness, based on core values.

A longstanding conundrum for leaders is whether or not good leaders show emotions. Tom Sergiovanni (1990) posited that showing outrage, for example, is an acceptable emotion for leaders. This was a very important lesson for me, because I had always heard that leaders in general, and women in particular, should never show emotions. People who showed emotions were considered to be unsuitable for leadership. And no one, especially a woman aspiring to leadership at the time, wanted to appear to be weak. That was certainly "career limiting," as it was often described.

This was validated in the early years of the "women in educational leadership" movement. Many of us were cautioned against showing negative emotions—especially anger. Some women certainly thought that they would never move up the organizational ladder if they did not comply. Even today, in many circles, the prevailing notion is that good leaders are never emotional.

Being emotional, especially when referring to women, is still viewed as a sign of weakness. In those prior days, it was particularly difficult for women who were thought to be too emotional to move up the leadership ladder. So many struggled with how they would be viewed if they allowed any emotion to become visible. But for me, Sergiovanni provided new ways of looking at this issue at the time. He made a convincing case that outrage is totally acceptable when important values are infringed upon. This resonated with me. It was one of the most liberating insights that I have had as an educational leader. It gave me permission to express outrage and to express it openly when deeply held universal values were compromised. Of course, with such behaviors, it always hinges on the question of *how* one expresses outrage or other emotions that are perceived as negative.

One answer lies in the ability to engage in constructive confrontation, which I learned through guidance and counseling courses and through assertiveness training. Being able to confront constructively means that it is never acceptable to express negative feelings at the expense of others. The language used is never intended to offend—to make ourselves feel good while putting others down. And although the term "confront" has such negative connotations, it is simply an invitation to others to see and appreciate the impact that their behavior is having on you or on others. Being able to confront constructively is an important interpersonal competency for all leaders.

Historically, we have seen debates in the literature on what exactly leadership means and how it is manifested. In the 1950s and 1960s, the *great-person* or *trait* approach to leadership suggested that leaders had a finite number of identifiable qualities—for example, charisma or integrity—which could be used to differentiate successful from unsuccessful leaders.

Later, the study of leaders concentrated on how leaders behaved—what they did, rather than how they appeared to others. This new focus gained popularity during the 1970s with the recognition that individual traits were significantly influenced by varying situations. This was described as *situational leadership*. However, many would say that the greatest failure of this approach was that it did not explain fully what leaders did, what they achieved, or the outcomes they forged.

A third categorization of leadership, *contingency leadership*, emerged in order to address the shortcomings of situational leadership. It is the view of Roueche, Baker, and Rose (1989) that among these perspectives, the notion of contingency leadership was the most comprehensive view of leadership at the time. They asserted,

> Underlying this approach is the idea that, to be effective, the leader must cause the internal functioning of the organization to be consistent with the demands of the organizational mission, technology or external environment, and to meet the needs of its various groups and members.

A major lesson that I have learned over the years is the fact that leaders must pay attention to, and seek to address, the needs of the people they lead. It is not unusual to see leaders booted out of office because they ignore people's needs or their sincere feedback on the directions that are being taken. Leaders who are self-absorbed often interpret this as criticism rather than valuable input for improvement. It sometimes seems as if leaders forget the people who elected or chose them in the first place. Still others forget the promises they made when they were actively seeking office. At the same time, I am by no means naive. People's needs and expectations change. Sometimes the demands are unachievable. The expectations may be inconsistent with one's values, out of step with the times, or incompatible with the philosophy and directions of the organization.

A case in point was in the early years when we fought to bring more women into administration. This was after many years of having leadership roles dominated by men, even though the profession was predominantly female. A few bold leaders sought to reverse this trend.

A vivid memory was a situation in which I worked as a young superintendent in a community described by many as conservative. At that time, many community members fought for the right to have input into who their principal would be. In this particular district, one of the demands was that they wanted a male principal. These were the early days of the women's movement in society in general, and in the educational arena in particular. But communities were not yet sensitized to these human rights issues. It took a lot of time to convince the members that we could not discriminate in this way. We also knew that if we sent a woman into that setting, she would have to overcome inordinate obstacles. We were able to convince the community about the superior qualifications and competence of the woman who was placed in that setting, and provided ongoing support for her transition. The following year, our criteria were carefully developed, with the caveat that it would not be appropriate to include the gender of the principal as one of the criteria for selection.

What Is Leadership Today?

Leadership is about making others better as a result of your presence and making sure that the impact lasts in your absence.

—*The Compelled Educator*, September 2014

Leadership is being bold enough to have vision and humble enough to recognize achieving it will take the efforts of many people—people who are most fulfilled when they share their gifts and talents, rather than just work. Leaders create that culture, serve that greater good and let others soar.

—Kathy Heasley, founder and president, Heasley & Partners (as cited in Helmrich, 2016)

We have spent half of our lives learning how to do, and teaching other people how to do. But we know in the end it is the quality and character of the leader that determines the performance—the results.

—Francis Hesselbein, former CEO of Girl Scouts of the USA (as cited in Chism, 2016)

Leadership is about making others better as a result of your presence and making sure that impact lasts in your absence.

—Sheryl Sandberg (2013)

Words like "direct" and "control" in early definitions of leadership reflect the authoritarianism of many leaders in the 1950s and 1960s. In the 1970s, situational leadership was the model style. In the 1980s and 1990s, terms such as "systems approach," "management by objectives," "participatory leadership," "transformational leadership," and "empowerment" became prevalent in the leadership literature. What we have also seen, with the progression of time, is a more humane, people-oriented, and human resources development approach to leadership and organizational improvement. Many leaders today recognize the importance of issues such as motivation in determining job satisfaction and productivity.

Admittedly, there are times when leaders must act authoritatively. Certain powers and authority are often given to leaders under our various acts, statutes, regulations, and strategic planning directions. A certain degree of accountability accompanies those responsibilities. But leaders today and in the future must have within their repertoire the leadership behaviors that engage people. They must become "enablers" creating conditions for employees to thrive and to do their best work. They must be able to develop the alliances and coalitions necessary to support their organizational goals. They must be able to work effectively with people to achieve the desired goals.

My image of the leader is one who has the competencies to motivate, inspire, and develop people. These leaders model positive character attributes. They are passionate about student achievement and the capacity building of staff. It is an image of a humane individual who provides strong advocacy to make the system work for the benefit of students and community. It is an individual who has within his or her repertoire an abundance of alternative dispute resolution (ADR) skills that enables him or her to arrive at win-win solutions when conflict arises. It is an image of responsive, dynamic, courageous, and optimistic leadership—one that eschews self-interest and is always thinking of what is in the interest of the common good.

As stated earlier, leadership requires a great deal of self-awareness, reflection, and analysis. The need for this orientation and related competencies cannot be overstated. It means that leaders must get in touch with their beliefs about human nature, because these beliefs affect profoundly one's leadership and management style. It means engaging in constant self-assessment to identify strengths, weaknesses, and areas that need improvement. By paying attention to these requirements, leaders set themselves on a pathway to achieving the highest levels of competence and professionalism.

The nature of leadership has also changed dramatically over the years. The cries for improved outcomes, higher standards, and increased accountability have become a worldwide phenomenon. Ever-expanding demands and expectations have placed new requirements on the role of the school leader. Within this milieu, many harken back to the words of Michael Fullan in his seminal book, *What's Worth Fighting For in the Principalship?* (1989). The following quote was a major source of inspiration for me as a young leader and continues to resonate in all aspects of leadership. Recognizing that we have the power to influence decisions and outcomes if we take action ourselves, rather than waiting on others to act, is a life lesson for those who aspire to be effective leaders:

> Counting on oneself for a good cause in a highly interactive organization is the key to fundamental organizational change. People change organizations. The starting point is not a system change, or change in those around us, but taking action ourselves. The challenge is to improve education in the only way it can be—through the day-to-day actions of empowered individuals. This is what's worth fighting for in the school principalship. (Fullan, 1989)

Michael Fullan expresses this imperative extremely well. The challenge is a timeless one with the potential for creating an enduring impact. It applies to leadership in all forums, in all settings, and at all stages along the career lifespan. It reinforces the importance of taking action ourselves to achieve desired results.

REACHING THE HEART OF LEADERSHIP: KEY REQUIREMENTS

In thinking about the content of this book, I have decided to focus on four leadership lessons that I have learned over almost forty years in education and the pivotal impact of these lessons on my thinking and leadership. Reducing this number to four was extremely difficult, as I have learned so many lessons across my professional lifespan.

I will describe briefly each of these lessons learned, review the literature on related research, and discuss some implications for leadership. These lessons are by no means unique to my experience. Leaders in both private- and public-sector institutions will attest to the fact that, when they consider their core business, many of the insights and experiences apply to themselves and their organizations as well. For that reason, I will assert that certain leadership qualities and practices can be found in all organizations. Most of the required competencies are also generalizable across occupational domains. In education, they must be in place if we are to reach the heart of leadership.

Reaching the heart of leadership therefore requires

- Self-knowledge and awareness;
- High expectations for learning and achievement;
- Holistic education: character, career, the arts, entrepreneurship; and
- Capacity building for system, school, and professional improvement.

Lessons Learned

1. Reaching the heart requires deep reflection and introspection about who we are and what we plan to achieve to ensure that our values and actions are aligned.

2. Respect is fundamental to healthy, effective, and productive relationships. It is one of the most important skills for us to demonstrate in the workplace.

3. It is necessary for leaders to find out what motivates their employees so that there is congruence between management expectations and employee understanding.

(Continued)

(Continued)

4. Empathy is the quintessential characteristic of human relationships. The ability to demonstrate this skill must be taught in leadership development programs.

5. Awareness of the difference between congeniality and collegiality as one's *modus operandi* in the workplace is essential for leaders. The former is necessary, but not sufficient. The latter can made a significant difference in achieving personal and organizational goals.

6. Human relations and interpersonal competency development are essential for aspiring and future leaders because of the pivotal role that these skills play in leadership effectiveness.

7. Conducting site visits to ask questions and compile a rounded picture of the attitudes and performance of aspiring leaders is a good way of balancing what people say in an interview and how they perform on their job—and, even more important, how they relate to people, especially those who are on the lower rungs of organizational ladders.

8. A clear understanding of issues such as power in general, and position power in particular, is critical for future leaders who need to be able to recognize the impact of their behavior on employees.

● ● ● ● ACTION STEPS FOR DEVELOPING EMPATHY

1. Establish a climate of respect, collaboration, high expectations, and good-will.

2. Provide ongoing professional learning opportunities for staff to increase self-knowledge and the importance of being reflective practitioners.

3. Help leaders and students learn motivation theory and seek to understand more fully the motivations behind the important decisions that are made.

4. Provide human relations and interpersonal competency training for staff and students.

5. Embed a strong human rights orientation in all policies, programs, and practices.

6. Review equity and inclusive education programs to encourage a strong social justice, fairness, and action orientation.

7. Implement leadership development programs for individuals at key stages along the leadership continuum.

8. Encourage future leaders to learn about their community by seeking out opportunities to become involved in outreach and engagement initiatives.

9. Develop partnerships with businesses, social agencies, community leaders, and politicians to strengthen school-community relationships.

10. Work with staff to ensure that their policies and practices best serve the needs of students.

11. Demonstrate continuous improvement in student learning, achievement, and well-being.

12. Learn about and address, within financial constraints, the reasonable expectations of community groups.

13. Work with parents, school councils, school districts, and other leaders to build consensus on the attributes that they want to have in their future leaders.

3

Self-Knowledge and Awareness

KNOW THYSELF!

As an educational leader, I have always recognized the importance of self-knowledge and awareness as an important skill in ensuring success in working with people. Philosophers who have influenced educational thought, such as Aristotle and Plato, have long exhorted us to "know thyself!" These skills help leaders first understand their own strengths and weaknesses and then move outward to begin to understand others more fully. Self-knowledge requires the ability to engage in deep introspection and reflection and a willingness to work at improving shortcomings.

As a leader, one of the most important tasks one has to perform is to select a team that will be effective in achieving the required outcomes. Leaders who have a high level of self-knowledge and awareness are better positioned to identify these skills and characteristics in others. This allows leaders to select a team that represents a wide range of attributes and skills. It also provides the insight that allows leaders to select a team that will complement their own skill set. And it helps leaders be more open to new and diverse ideas. That is why studies of executives in a variety of industries, both public and private, have found that high self-awareness is the strongest predictor of leadership effectiveness (Flaum, 2010; Tjan, Harrington, & Hsieh, 2012).

To become more self-aware, leaders need to be reflective about their own attributes and leadership practices (Coombs, 2001). They need to know what motivates them and what influences their decision making. However, they must then go beyond personal reflection and also develop sensitivity to the values and orientations of others, so that they can give meaning to the actions of those they lead (Begley, 2006).

The inside-out approach is a very effective strategy for those who want to grow in knowledge of what guides and motivates their thinking, values, and actions. There are a number of variables that one should consider in that personal quest for increased self-awareness. These include examining one's

a) Values, beliefs, attitudes, and dispositions

b) Beliefs about human nature

c) Biases and prejudices

d) Ability and willingness to make moral and ethical decisions

Our core values, beliefs, attitudes, and dispositions influence how we see the world, our actions, and the decisions we make. These are often formed over one's lifetime, beginning in early childhood. They are the sum total of all our experiences and relationships with significant others.

Those values, beliefs, and attitudes may also ultimately influence the decisions leaders are called upon to make in their boardrooms, schools, and districts.

It is very important for leaders to become increasingly aware of their values in particular. They need to be aware of the source of these values and how they manifest themselves in interactions with others. Greater self-awareness should help us become more accepting of the diverse perspectives of the members of our teams—especially in multicultural and multiracial contexts. The ability of a leader to deal effectively with diversity is a major source of success (or failure) during these times of heightened awareness of—and commitment to—human rights issues. A lack of sensitivity to the values of the people we lead can be detrimental to our leadership success. One example of this is an incident I discussed earlier in this book, about the principal who was "run out of town" because it was felt that she did not take seriously the prevailing values of her rural community. This was all about the importance of getting to know deeply held community values.

Being aware of one's dispositions or temperament is also essential, as the people we lead can be affected by our moods. People often say that when they walk into a school, they can sense immediately what the climate of the school is and the tone that the leader has set for the organization. A leader who is self-aware has a high level of self-regulation, ensuring that employees are not affected negatively by the leader's feelings, moods, or behaviors. Goleman, Boyatzis, and McKee (2002) also discuss this leadership skill.

Our beliefs about human nature also influence how we lead. Douglas McGregor's Theory X and Theory Y, discussed in his book *The Human Side of the Enterprise* (1960), which influenced my early thinking about human nature at work, illustrate this point fully. In a nutshell, Theory X states that people are basically lazy, unambitious, unmotivated, irresponsible, selfish, and not very smart. Theory Y, on the other hand, describes people as energetic, motivated, ambitious, responsible, selfless, self-directed, and intelligent. These theories represent negative and positive views of human nature, respectively. If these theories influence leadership behaviors in the workplace, the leader's theoretical orientation can have a powerful impact on how leaders behave—for example, on tasks such as participatory problem solving.

In addition, William Ouchi (1981) popularized Theory Z, based on the work of W. Edwards Deming. He came to prominence by pointing out the differences between Japanese and American companies and management styles. It is interesting that he also wrote about how to make schools more effective.

Theory Z is essentially people-oriented in its pronouncements. It focuses on issues such as well-being and loyalty. Ouchi favored stability in employment, high productivity, and high employee morale. He once said that

> The secret of Japanese success is not technology, but a special way of managing people—a style that focusses on strong company philosophy, a distinct corporate culture, long-range staff development and consensus decision-making. (Ouchi, 1981)

It goes without saying that if we believe in and are guided by the tenets of Theory Y, our leadership behaviors would be drastically different from those who believe in Theory X. In fact, I have worked with leaders whose leadership characteristics I can easily subsume under each of these headings. What was most interesting and instructive for me were the lessons learned and insights gained about leadership when I worked with supervisors who demonstrated each of these orientations. I knew instinctively whom I did not want to emulate or be like—the style I did not want to possess.

Throughout my career, I have been vehement in my denunciation of Theory X leadership. In the past, I remember challenging one of my "bosses" who demonstrated these qualities. This confrontation could have cost me my career. But what I believe helped was the language I used, having taken assertiveness training early in my career. Suffice it to that the Theory X orientation is so detrimental to employee health, well-being, and productivity that organizations should offer courses and coaching to prospective leaders when they see evidence of a strong Theory X orientation. Or, better still, if Theory X individuals do not demonstrate a significant change of heart and behavior, they should not be promoted to positions in which they are expected to manage or lead people.

If organizations do not take action and retrain or weed out individuals without strong people skills, they will certainly have to pay later for the leadership mistakes, missteps, and overall ineffectiveness of Theory X leaders. When a prospective leader has a negative view of human nature and does not have a strong people-orientation, leadership selection processes should take these shortcomings seriously to protect the morale of employees and the culture of the organization.

During and after the 1975 International Women's Year, some of us were sensitized to women in leadership issues. There was ample evidence of discrimination that resulted in female aspirants' lack of access to principals' training programs, promotion processes, and leadership roles. To see this, one just had to look at the number of women in the teaching profession in most countries, especially at the elementary or primary level, compared to the number of women in educational leadership.

Some of us wanted to experience what it would be like to work with women leaders as our supervisors. I had a great epiphany and, as a consequence, learned a very important lesson at that time— one that remained with me throughout my career—that gender was not the most important quality in determining leadership effectiveness. I wanted so much to believe that was the case, but my experience gave me a more balanced view of who the effective leaders were and the qualities that such leaders possessed.

It was surprising and somewhat ironic that the leader I admired most at the time was a male principal with whom I worked as a vice principal. He was the most caring, sincere, empathetic, trusting, and positive individual with whom I had ever interacted in the workplace! It jarred all my stereotypes of male leadership and debunked all the myths I had imbibed during those years. That was a great experience for me, as it reinforced the fact that the positive leadership qualities that I am identifying in this book resided in both males and females. What this insight meant for me was the need to ensure that we demonstrate fidelity to upholding the values of fairness and equity when we assume leadership roles. After all, these were the values for which we had fought all those years.

After this experience, I refocused my attention on being a role model and mentor for both young women and young men, while recognizing fully that there were still personal and organizational biases that gave males the advantage for leadership roles. At the time, I remember being struck by the statistics on the number of women teachers in Ontario and elsewhere, compared to the number of women in educational administration. The disparity was still great. There was still a need to have special programs to attract and retain women in leadership roles.

I do recall an incident, as superintendent of schools, when, in a particular year, all the individuals who were promoted were female. This happened when visiting a school one day, and I was accosted by a young man. The young man was very upset, and stated that he had applied to become a vice principal and yet the entire short list that year was female. He wondered aloud if this was about "women's lib." He mentioned the name of a woman in his school who had also applied and was placed on the short list. I sat down with him and tried to encourage him not to give up. He referred to this woman again. I asked him a few questions: "How many years of experience do you have?"

"Five," he said. (This was the minimum number of years one needed as a teacher to apply for leadership.)

"In how many divisions has she taught?" I asked.

"She has taught in three divisions," he replied. Teaching in three divisions was a requirement to apply to be an elementary vice principal in Ontario, among other requirements. This could include the primary (Grades K–3), the junior (Grades 4–6), the intermediate (Grades 7–10), or the senior (Grades 11–12) divisions.

Aside from the issue of qualifications, the most telling response was this one. When I asked how much preparation he had done for the interview, his response was that he had not prepared much for the interview. He wanted to know what I meant by "preparing" for an interview. Little did he know that the women had formed study groups and were meeting for months before the interview—going over past and anticipated questions, conducting mock interviews, and assisting one another with model answers. I would guess that women would feel compelled to engage in these activities because, in the early days, women knew they had to work twice as hard as men did for whatever they wanted to achieve. Nothing would be given to them on a platter.

I invited this young man and a few others who were interviewed to meet with me and gave them some practice in preparing for interviews and answering questions. Later on, we assisted all individuals who were thinking of applying for promotions in practicing job-interview skills as a part of a larger leadership development program, which had a designated strand for aspiring leaders.

As I reflected on this experience, I realized that, indeed, the women's movement generated many programs to assist women who wanted to assume leadership roles. It was needed because biases were still prevalent. We did not have many role models who had traveled that road. But one also had to admit that young men did not have many opportunities to prepare in a formal and transparent way.

Some of my friends said that my empathy for these young men was misplaced. The number of men in leadership roles was still disproportionate to their numbers at lower levels of the organizational hierarchy. My friends were convinced that men were mentored in different ways—on the golf course, on the sports field, and in other organizations of which men were members and to which the women were not privy. Admittedly, that was the case. But as an educational leader who wrote equity and inclusive policies, it was important to be a mentor for both men and women. If one considers oneself to be a transformational leader, one cannot fight for changes and then later erect barriers that resemble the obstacles that one fought hard to dismantle. If a leader behaves in this way, he or she would, at best, be disingenuous. A certain level of self-monitoring is necessary to achieve congruence between values and behavior.

As an immigrant to Canada, it was also important for me to provide strong advocacy to ensure that more individuals from diverse communities had pathways established for them to get into leadership positions. Students need to see a strong representation of diversity of their communities in educational leadership. If this is not the case, they will not trust what we say about equity and inclusivity. In other words, they would tell us that we are not practicing what we are preaching. The statement "Your actions speak so loudly that I can hardly hear what you are saying" is applicable in these situations.

Admittedly, much remains to be done. But those in leadership in many of our Canadian provinces and parts of the United States do not yet represent the diversity of the larger communities. One just has to attend a meeting of principals or superintendents to see how homogeneous the senior management groups are. But I remain optimistic. I do not doubt that there is commitment in many districts to improve this situation. What is most obvious to me is the desire of senior management teams—regardless of their composition—to redouble current efforts to improve the life chances of students in general, and of children from poor or diverse communities in particular.

The aspect that concerns me most, and one that I have shared openly in many settings, is the fact that when students from diverse background see members of senior staff as a team, they do not see individuals with whom they instantly identify. Having role models who look like oneself is very important, given the diversity that exists in the broader society. From a career development perspective, we want our students to look to our leaders and say, "I could be like her," or "I could be like him." If they do not have these role models, they may not aspire to these roles, as I discovered in my study of the career aspirations and expectations of Ontario high school girls.

Ontario, for example, launched an equity and inclusive education strategy, which is still being implemented at this time. I was fortunate enough to be a co-chair of the committee that developed this strategy. Premier Kathleen Wynne was education minister at the time. Under her leadership, and at her insistence, Ontario developed and continues to implement the equity strategy that is still an important part of government policy in education.

This strategy document can be accessed here: http://www.edu.gov .on.ca/eng/policyfunding/equity.pdf.

The work of the minister of education, the Honorable Karen Casey, and her team in Nova Scotia deserve special commendation. They have developed an action plan that includes strategies to improve the education of Nova Scotians of African descent. I was fortunate to have had the opportunity to participate in a few of their processes as well. In one of the activities, we convened a group of key community leaders and organizations to

- Identify what they are doing well;
- Find common ground on the priorities among the key organizations to address the achievement and well-being of African Nova Scotian children;
- Prioritize what remains to be done;
- Develop an action plan;
- Determine the supports;
- Engage key partners and organizations;
- Forge a commitment to build the necessary coalitions; and
- Harness the supports necessary to bring about change.

It was necessary, as in all initiatives, to identify the research-informed approaches that contribute to improvement and to build capacity among staff to improve teaching, learning, and leadership. The primary goal of the Nova Scotian government is to improve student achievement and well-being. The stated intent of the minister's recent education strategy document, *The 3Rs: Renew, Refocus, Rebuild*, is to help change the learning and teaching environment. This strategy can be accessed through this link: http://www.ednet .ns.ca/education-actionplan.

PERIPHERAL VISION AND RECOGNITION OF FUTURE TRENDS

A core characteristic of effective leaders is the ability to have a vision of a preferred future, to identify smart goals, and to articulate these goals clearly to their staff so that they know the role they are expected to play in achieving that vision (Wilhelm, 1996, p. 223). All successful leadership starts with a vision, as leaders must set out a "compelling image of an achievable future" (Friedman, 2009). A clear vision works both to inspire and to focus attention and efforts on what is most important. A necessary component of this is to constantly scan the environment for trends, opportunities, and challenges that would thwart one's quest to fulfill that vision. Consistent with the literature on contextual leadership, leaders today require an understanding of a range of factors that are both internal and external to the organization (House & Aditya, 1997).

One of my early insights as a leader was the importance of having a clear vision of what we wanted to achieve. The leaders whom I admired most in my early years were those who had an inspiring vision of where they wanted to take the organization. They had a sense of what the school or organization should look like and, more important, how to get there. Authentic collaboration with colleagues was essential if they were to make a real difference in the lives of the people they chose to serve.

I have always thought that having visions but not a pathway toward achieving them is empty chatter. People lose confidence in talk with no accompanying action. What is important is that a leader possesses certain skills and competencies for the execution of seemingly lofty ideas. A leader must know how to coopt others so that they buy into the leader's dream or image of the future. Leaders have to realize that they cannot do things alone, and that what is important is to influence and convince others to assume ownership and to be willing to put in the hard work required to achieve the goals.

One of the lessons I have learned is that visions can, indeed, be lofty. What is important is that they must be accompanied by intentionality, focused action, and competent execution. From my experience, visionary leaders certainly became the beacon of hope for the future we all wanted to achieve together. These leaders had a vision for the future, but, more important, they were able to tap into the vision of others, integrate their ideas and aspirations, and translate the notions into a combined vision for the future. It meant that when individuals recited the vision and mission statements, they could see themselves, their aspirations, and their role in that vision and in its realization. This helped build commitment and loyalty—essential qualities for organizational cohesion.

Reaching the heart of leadership requires that aspiring and current leaders learn about future trends so that they are not taken by surprise or derailed from their course. The fact that we are engaged in preparing students for a future that we cannot fully imagine is another reason for paying attention to these trends.

Educators, because of the very nature of their work, must have a keen interest in the futurist literature. The trends that I have found most helpful in working with teachers are those proposed by Gary Marx, who has conducted trends research for more than fifty years. He has worked with businesses and countries across the world. For years, Marx proposed sixteen trends. His most recent research identified twenty-one trends.

● ● ● ● FUTURE TRENDS IN EDUCATION

(Gary Marx, 2014)

1. **Generations:** Millennials will insist on solutions to accumulated problems and injustices and will profoundly impact leadership and lifestyles.

2. **Diversity:** In a series of tipping points, majorities will become minorities, creating ongoing challenges for social cohesion.

3. **Aging:** In developed nations, the old will generally outnumber the young. In developing nations, the young will generally outnumber the old.

4. **Technology:** Ubiquitous, interactive technologies will shape how we live, how we learn, how we see ourselves, and how we relate to the world.

5. **Identity and privacy:** Identity and privacy issues will lead to an array of new and often urgent concerns and a demand that they be resolved.

6. **Economy:** An economy for a new era will demand restoration and reinvention of physical, social, technological, educational, and policy infrastructure.

(Continued)

(Continued)

7. **Jobs and careers:** Pressure will grow for society to prepare people for jobs and careers that may not currently exist.

8. **Energy:** The need to develop new sources of affordable and accessible energy will lead to intensified scientific invention and political tension.

9. **Environmental/planetary security:** Common opportunities and threats will intensify a worldwide demand for planetary security.

10. **Sustainability:** Sustainability will depend on adaptability and resilience in a fast-changing, at-risk world.

11. **International/global education:** International learning—including relationships, cultural understanding, languages, and diplomatic skills—will become basic.

    a. **Sub-trend:** To earn respect in an interdependent world, nations will be expected to demonstrate their reliability and tolerance.

12. **Personalization:** In a world of diverse talents and aspirations, we will increasingly discover and accept that one size does not fit all.

13. **Ingenuity:** Releasing ingenuity and stimulating creativity will become primary responsibilities of education and society.

14. **Depth, breadth, and purposes of education:** The breadth, depth, and purposes of education will constantly be clarified to meet the needs of a fast-changing world.

15. **Polarization:** Polarization and narrowness will, of necessity, bend toward reasoned discussion, evidence, and consideration of varying points of view.

16. **Authority:** A spotlight will fall on how people gain authority and use it.

17. **Ethics:** Scientific discoveries and societal realities will force widespread ethical choices.

18. **Continuous improvement:** The status quo will yield to continuous improvement and reasoned progress.

19. **Poverty:** Understanding will grow that sustained poverty is expensive, debilitating, and unsettling.

20. **Scarcity versus abundance:** Scarcity will help us rethink our view of abundance.

21. **Personal meaning and work-life balance:** More of us will seek personal meaning in our lives in response to an intense, high-tech, always on, fast-moving society.

My longstanding interest in the trends research began when I was a classroom teacher. I remember hearing a statement that stayed with me over the years: "The future belongs to those who can see it coming!"

Statistics tell us that many of the young people with whom we are working today will have working lives of more than forty years after graduation. Even though trends may change, knowing what they are now will help us prepare children for the future, however uncertain it may be. Trends provide us with glimpses over the horizon and into the future. They tell us that our graduates will have to deal with many challenges, changing landscapes, patterns, opportunities, expectations, and needs. They help us understand the pitfalls and the possibilities that we will encounter in our work and daily lives. By studying them, we can anticipate impacts and give our students the knowledge, skills, attitudes, and dispositions to deal with the unknown. Most important, we can prepare students and ourselves to become solution finders locally, nationally, and internationally.

MORAL AND ETHICAL DECISION MAKING

Over the past two decades, in light of many leaders' scandals that have occurred in both the public and the private sectors, there has been increased attention paid to the moral and ethical dimensions of leadership (Den Hartog, 2015). Ethical leadership is now seen as absolutely crucial to a leader's ability to inspire and influence others (Brown, Trevino, & Harrison, 2005; Piccolo, Greenbaum, Den Hartog, & Folger, 2010). One definition of *ethical leadership* is "the demonstration of normatively appropriate conduct through personal actions and interpersonal relationships, and the promotion of such conduct to followers through two-way communication, reinforcement, and decision-making" (Brown et al., 2005, p. 120). Ethical leaders are therefore "humble, concerned for the greater good, strive for fairness, take responsibility and show respect for each individual" (Mihelic, Lipicnik, & Tekavcic, 2010, p. 31).

Ethical leadership is not just a moral obligation; it has also been shown to improve performance and effectiveness within organizations (Piccolo et al., 2010; Walumbwa, Morrison, & Christensen, 2012). Furthermore, ethical leadership has been found to increase satisfaction with the leader and perceptions of leader effectiveness, as well as followers' job dedication and well-being, and has been found to decrease cynicism within organizations (Hassan, Mahsud, Yuki, & Prussia, 2013; Kalshoven & Boon, 2012; Neubert, Carlson, Kacmar, Roberts, & Chonko, 2009). And perhaps not surprisingly, other research has shown that ethical leadership increases prosocial behavior and decreases the unethical conduct of others within organizations (Brown & Trevino, 2006).

The failure of a few leaders in recent years has created some skepticism and mistrust within organizations. Leaders are finding, more than ever, that they have to prove themselves each day. They are fully aware that trust is essential to their effectiveness. They must now prove that they are deserving of that trust.

Interestingly, though, I have read that companies such as Enron and Tyco that were in serious trouble for what has been described as unethical activities have beautifully written beliefs-and-values statements adorning the walls of their organizations.

The Enron scandal, revealed in October 2001, was described as the largest bankruptcy reorganization in American history at that time, as well as the biggest audit failure. Executives were indicted for a variety of charges, and some were later sentenced. This, for me, was a clear lesson on the importance of leaders' practicing what they preach, being transparent, and being genuinely ethical in their values, beliefs, and behaviors.

BIASES, STEREOTYPES, AND PREJUDICES

In the early years of the women's movement, stereotyping was a favorite topic for us to talk about. Stereotypes abound for all groups. What is sad is that some groups are consistently stereotyped positively, while others are consistently portrayed in a negative way. Some people will defend this practice, referring to those who "complain" as "overly sensitive," and will say that stereotypes are innocuous. These individuals are often quite dismissive, of those who complain about this inconsistency, offering the explanation that all groups are stereotyped.

I was particularly interested in understanding the issue of prejudice and discrimination more fully in my early years as a teacher. I could understand the tendency to stereotype—I am sure that I was guilty of this behavior as well. But I have always recognized the devastating impact that stereotyping can have if, as educators, we do not guard against it in our work with students. Most educators learn about the Pygmalion effect and its corollary, the Golem effect, in teacher's college. These are self-fulfilling prophecies. With the former, we attribute higher expectations, which lead to increased performance. With the latter, we attribute low expectations, which lead to decreased performance.

This phenomenon has also been attributed to leadership expectations. What we do know is that expectations matter and that leaders must be aware of the expectations we have of all those who fall within our sphere of influence. Even more important, those who work with young people must never place limits on what they are capable of doing or achieving. They will always surprise us. At parties, when we mention that we are educators, so many stories are told with great resentment: "My teachers said I would amount to nothing," or "My principal said I would just be a school dropout," or "I was told, 'You are just as lazy as your brother; you will never be able to do math well!'"

A colleague sent me a photograph of a high jumper with one leg— Arnold Boldt, who lives in Saskatchewan, Canada. Boldt defies all predictions about his ability and surprises everyone because he

Never underestimate a student's potential!

continues to exceed all expectations. (You can see a video of Boldt in action at http://www.youtube.com/watch?v=H82kwz9S3Xg.)

There is a clear message for us as educators when we work with students. We should never underestimate their ability. They will continue to surprise us!

As a teacher, it was very important for me to make every effort to ensure that stereotypes about the children I taught were not harbored—especially about their ability. This is necessary because stereotypes do reside in all our minds—even with the best of intentions. And what is even more disconcerting is that these judgments can surreptitiously affect how we relate to students, how we evaluate them, and how we make decisions about their lives.

Against my better judgment, and even though I do not want to prejudge situations, I have been tempted to categorize people because of how they dress, how they speak, or their demeanor. I nearly gave up on my quest to be free of biases when I was told a story that was going around for years at the time to illustrate the pervasiveness of stereotyping. This riddle went something like this:

> A man and his son are driving in a car one day, when they get into a fatal accident. The man is killed instantly. The boy is knocked unconscious, but he is still alive. He is rushed to hospital, requiring immediate surgery. The doctor enters the emergency room, looks at the boy, and says, *"I can't operate on this boy! I can't operate on my own son."*

The question is, how do you explain this? How it this possible?

The answer, of course, is that the doctor is the boy's mother. It is amazing how many people who thought they were free of biases and stereotypes could not get the answer. Many wondered aloud, "Was this a case of reincarnation?" They just could not explain this, because their minds were stuck on the notion that the doctor was a man. Even I failed this test! It taught me how powerful conditioning is in controlling our minds and our thinking, and taught me the importance of humility in dealing with issues such as our propensity to think stereotypically.

On the question of prejudice, we would also deny vociferously that we have any prejudices, because, for us, it is anathema. After all, we are fair people! But, again, close scrutiny reveals that we have learned many prejudices over our lifetime. The solution is simply to acknowledge them and their source, and think of what needs to be done to monitor our behavior, especially toward those who are different from us.

There are many implications and lessons to be learned about prejudice and the human proclivity toward stereotyping others—both individuals and groups. This phenomenon can lead to overt or covert expressions of prejudice and discrimination. Many years ago, Gordon Allport (1979), a Harvard psychologist, in his seminal work on the nature of prejudice, provided insight into this problem. He offered recommendations on how to reduce the devastating effects of prejudice on individuals and society. And although numerous books have been written in the interim, Allport's book is a must read for all those who want to have a deep understanding of this issue.

As educators, instead of thinking that we are free of stereotypes, it is important to accept the fact that we have not escaped conditioning—by our families, television, the books we read, and other media—and to work hard at overcoming our prejudices and to avoid acting on them. We will be able to reach the heart of leadership only by paying assiduous attention to this critical aspect of interpersonal understanding and interactions. It means working hard to become more aware of our own conditioning, and developing strategies to decrease our tendency to stereotype and categorize others.

LEADERSHIP IS POLITICAL!

While the word "politics" can conjure up negative associations, the reality is that all organizations are inherently political (Mintzberg, 1985). Schools are no different. Therefore, being an effective leader involves acknowledging this political reality and engaging with it skillfully. In this context, a common definition of *political skill* is the ability to understand and influence others in order to accomplish organizational objectives (Ahearn, Ferris, Hockwarter, Douglas, & Ammeter, 2004). Ferris and colleagues (2005) outline four dimensions of political skill:

- **Social astuteness:** Individuals possessing political skill are astute observers of others and are keenly attuned to diverse social situations. They comprehend social interactions and accurately interpret their own behavior, as well as that of others, in social settings. They have strong powers of discernment and high self-awareness.

- **Interpersonal influence:** Politically skilled individuals have a subtle and convincing personal style that exerts a powerful influence on those around them. Individuals with high interpersonal influence, nonetheless, are capable of appropriately adapting and calibrating their behavior to each situation in order to elicit particular responses from others.

- **Networking ability:** Individuals with strong political skill are adept at developing and using diverse networks of people. People in these networks tend to hold assets seen as valuable and necessary for successful personal and organizational functioning. By the sheer force of their typically subtle style, politically skilled individuals easily develop friendships and build strong, beneficial alliances and coalitions.

- **Apparent sincerity:** Politically skilled individuals appear to others as possessing high levels of integrity, authenticity, sincerity, and genuineness. They are, or appear to be, honest, open, and forthright.

These competencies—social astuteness, interpersonal influence, networking ability, and apparent sincerity—are essential for leadership today. They symbolize the head, the heart, and the hands—words commonly used to describe the cognitive, affective, and behavioral domains of learning. The ability to demonstrate astuteness, sincerity, and influence should be taught in all leadership development programs. Without these essential prerequisites, leaders will not be able to develop trust—the *sine qua non* of leadership and a major conduit to the heart.

Interestingly, these are described as the "soft skills." I am convinced that the soft skills are, indeed, the hard skills. They must be taught systematically. They are not learned by osmosis or association with those who possess these 21st century skills.

There is also reason to believe that educational leaders have a particular obligation to engage with the broader political system, as it affects their ability to initiate and lead positive educational change. For example, Lammel (2000) states that leaders in education "have a moral responsibility to stand up and be counted on those issues that affect quality education for all students" (p. 2).

This means that leaders must be willing to engage in positive political action, utilizing the influencing skills we have honed over the years and making sure that schools best serve the needs of students. This positive form of politics is simply about marshaling all resources available—human, financial, and material—to influence decisions about children and their needs. By taking action to benefit students, we reach the heart of leadership.

----- Leadership Lessons Learned

1. It has been said that leaders hire and promote in their own image. It is necessary to disrupt this trend and to create diverse teams to support the need of people and the organization.

2. Larry Lazotte once said, "If you can find an effective school without a successful principal, call me collect." Throughout the course of my career, this has proven to be a truism.

(Continued)

(Continued)

3. It is essential to gather information from the individuals you supervise in order to have a good picture of how you are perceived and how your actions affect their daily lives.

4. Leaders require different skills and leadership development along the continuum from aspiring leaders to experienced leaders.

5. Learning about trends are important; remember the saying "the future belongs to those who can see it coming," and that we must be cognizant of the pitfalls and possibilities.

6. Educating young people to be global citizens and solution finders means paying attention to trends and what is happening across the globe.

7. It is important for leaders to practice what they preach; their credibility and trustworthiness depend on this.

8. Understanding the politics of education and issues such as power, privilege, and influence is key to success in educational leadership.

● ● ● ● ACTION STEPS FOR LEADING ETHICALLY

1. Work at selecting a diverse team that represents a wide array of attributes and skills and that balances the skills that you do not have.

2. Provide opportunities to develop sensitivity to the values and orientation of your staff and community.

3. Provide systematic outreach to the community to learn about the values and priorities of your diverse populations and to seek out their perspectives and guidance. Ensure that they are represented and that their voices are heard on key committees.

4. Develop a leadership program with varied experiences along the leadership continuum to differentiate and personalize the requirements.

5. Develop a succession plan that includes a future leaders program to attract and train a diverse group of individuals who will replace your current cohort.

6. Work with your team to remove barriers to access for under-represented groups; provide career guidance, role models, and strong advocacy to disrupt current patterns of identification and selection of future leaders if your system is not becoming more diverse.

7. Visit and learn from other systems, such as Ontario and Nova Scotia, who are embedding equity and inclusive education programs.

8. Develop a vision of a preferred future after scanning your environment, anticipating the trends and the internal and external factors that could derail your progress.

9. Ensure that leadership development programs include the teaching of "soft skills," human relations training, and interpersonal dynamics, as these are essential skills in working effectively with people.

4

High Expectations for Learning and Achievement

It has long been known that people do better when more is expected of them. Considerable empirical evidence has shown that higher expectations lead to increased student performance, dubbed the *Pygmalion effect* (Alviridez & Weinstein, 1999; de Boer, Bosker, & van der Werf, 2010; Jussim & Harber, 2005). Conversely, there is a large body of evidence showing that having low expectations negatively affects the learning of students (Brophy, 1983; Brophy & Good, 1970; Cooper & Good, 1983; Kuklinski & Weinstein, 2000; St. George, 1983; Weinstein, 2002). This is because "when we expect certain behaviors of others, we are more likely to act in ways that make the expected behavior more likely to occur" (Rosenthal & Babad, 1985, p. 36). The importance of creating a culture of high expectations cannot be overstated, as it has been shown to be one of the most powerful ways to increase student learning and achievement (Hattie, 2009).

For years, Michael Fullan, an international icon in education, asserted the following:

> The new mission for schools is to achieve 90 to 95 percent success. This is what it will take for societies to thrive in the complex world of the 21st century. (Fullan, Hill, & Crevola, 2006)

Fullan and colleagues also said,

> The new mission takes over where the old one left off. It is to get *all* students to meet high standards of education and to provide them with a lifelong education that does not have the built-in obsolescence of so much old-style curriculum but that equips them to be lifelong learners.
>
> (Fullan, Hill, & Crevola, 2006)

A couple of years ago, I had a discussion with Fullan and asked him if his views on this topic had changed. His response was,

> The new mission of schools is to achieve 100% success and to have specific explanations and strategies for addressing any figure that falls short of full success. (Fullan, personal communication, 2015)

Others, like Schleicher and Stewart (2008), identified the key features of high-performing countries as well. These include the following:

- High universal standards
- Accountability and autonomy
- Strengthened teacher professionalism
- Personalized learning

One of the reasons for the success experienced in the Ontario strategy was the recognition that if we were going achieve excellence and equity, it was necessary to establish ambitious targets for our students. Along with the targets, we looked deeply into what the behavioral correlates of developing a culture of high expectations for all students and staff looked like.

High expectations for students success included the following:

- Creating a culture that puts students at the center of all decision making
- Establishing ambitious targets
- Communicating expectations regularly
- Focusing and building on students' strengths and assets
- Providing models of expected performance
- Rejecting negative stereotypes and a focus on deficits
- Having a schoolwide commitment to continuous improvement
- Developing higher-order thinking and analytical skills
- Personalizing instruction
- Sharing examples of exemplary work
- Engaging students in goal setting and assessment practice
- Providing early intervention and ongoing supports
- Being demanding
- Developing a culture of "no excuses"

Over the course of my career, it has been my conviction that having high expectations is one of the most important contributions that we can make in educating students. Having high expectations is, in essence, an equity issue. During the student forum at the Quest Conference in the York Region District School Boards a few years ago, a student said, "The best gift you can give me is your high expectations for me."

As a first step, principals and teachers need to communicate to their students the belief that they can all achieve at high levels. In schools that have developed a culture of high expectations, student achievement and success are celebrated on a regular basis. The atmosphere is demanding, but students are having fun learning, because they are being stretched to reach their potential. Students are given exemplars of what good work looks like and are encouraged to measure their work against those standards. The focus is on tasks that require higher-order thinking and analytical skills.

High expectations must also permeate all classroom activities. Educators today must believe that all children can learn and achieve, given time and proper supports. If this is the case, those beliefs must be explicit and pervasive and must be made visible in schools and classrooms. Educators must be totally committed in their efforts to push the boundaries and do all that is within their reach to make success become a reality for all students.

And when one visits these schools and classrooms in which educators say they have a culture of high expectations for all, there should be examples of characteristics that are commonly discussed within education circles, for example.

● ● ● ● HOW TO PERPETUATE A CULTURE OF HIGH EXPECTATIONS

Principals should

- Establish a schoolwide commitment to continuous improvement
- Set ambitious targets that are monitored regularly
- Determine the character attributes that will form the basis of behavior and interactions through a collaborative process with the community
- Establish a common understanding of what high expectations look like
- Provide early interventions and supports for struggling students, including tutoring, after-school programs, and summer programs
- Develop intrinsic motivation, encouraging students to do their best work
- Assist parents with strategies on how they can help their children succeed
- Celebrate successes regularly, in all domains of learning

Teachers should

- Personalize instruction to meet the unique needs and interests of their students

- Share examples of exemplary work, including anchor charts and performance walls
- Provide regular opportunities for purposeful talk and meaningful discussions and interactions
- Engage in problem-based learning
- Facilitate design thinking strategies
- Provide opportunities across all subject areas to develop higher-order thinking and analytical skills
- Include opportunities for students to develop creativity and entrepreneurship
- Develop and share exemplars of what good work looks like

Students should

- Set high standards for learning and high expectations for achievement
- Have opportunities to revise their work so that they learn to improve on what they have written
- Engage in discussions about what the next steps should be in their learning process
- Be encouraged to take increasing responsibility for their own learning

Parents should

- Feel welcomed in the school
- Help develop the academic, attitudinal, and behavioral standards that are expected
- Have opportunities for meaningful involvement
- Have regular communication and be kept informed about the progress of their children
- Help determine the mechanism to provide regular feedback on policies, programs, and interactions
- Learn about the ways they can contribute to their children's learning

EQUITABLE AND INCLUSIVE SCHOOLS FOR *ALL* LEARNERS

Apart from a focus on issues related to justice, there are several social and economic reasons for societies to be concerned about equity (Gaskell & Levin, 2012). For example, there is increased recognition that inequality is linked to reduced social cohesion, which is in turn linked to poorer economic growth and less ability to attract investors (Green, Preston, & Janmaat, 2006; Lloyd-Ellis, 2003; Osberg, 1995). Furthermore, there is growing evidence that countries with less inequality tend to have better economic and social outcomes (Wilkinson & Pickett, 2009). This brings together the seemingly disparate social and economic arguments for reduced inequity.

Making schools more equitable has become a major mandate for governments across the globe. In the past, equity conversations have tended to focus on achievement gaps, as measured by standardized test scores. However, Ladson-Billings (2006), past president of the American Educational Research Association, argues that the achievement gap is a logical consequence of the "education debt," a collection of the historical, economic, sociopolitical, and moral debts accrued against marginalized and racialized peoples and children. Thus, she states, effectively addressing the achievement gap must involve first addressing the education debt.

In a similar vein, there is growing recognition that achievement gaps in schools are heavily influenced by the opportunity gaps that students from traditionally marginalized backgrounds have faced. Opportunity gaps can be conceptualized in terms of three dimensions of inequality (Fraser, 2005). These are

- Inequality in the material conditions of children's lives
- Denial of cultural belonging or equal social status
- An inequitable voice in decisions that affect one's well-being

This means that our idea of equity needs to move beyond equitable student achievement to include other outcomes, such as student experiences, discussions about their lives and the conditions that affect them on a daily basis, student engagement and well-being, and opportunities for students and their families to have a voice in the decisions that affect them. To this end, school systems should regularly collect various forms of large-scale student data— on student engagement, well-being, and achievement, to name a few—and disaggregate these data by social demographics to identify gaps in opportunity, experience, treatment, well-being, and achievement. In addition, while is it usually accepted that one of the purposes of education is to produce engaged citizens, equitable education requires that democratic practices be built directly into school structures, so as to promote critical democracy as a way of life (Glass, 2007).

Breaking Barriers: Excellence and Equity for All, by Glaze, Mattingley, and Levin (2012), identifies twenty-one strategies to close achievement gaps and concrete ideas to address these issues at all levels of the education system. We offer practical ideas for administrators and teachers to break down the barriers that can truncate the life chances of students. As mentioned earlier, the work being done in provinces such as Ontario and those proposed by the Nova Scotia Department of Education, among other Canadian provinces, provide some promising practices.

- - - - - Leadership Lessons Learned

1. Creating a culture of high expectations for learning and achievement is an essential task of all educators, to ensure that all children, regardless of background or personal circumstance, achieve.

2. We can no longer accept the fact that a certain number of children will fail. Fullan's imperative that the new mission of school is for 100 percent success is the new bar.

3. There is widespread agreement on the key features of high-performing schools. Behavioral correlates of these levels of expected achievement must be established and promulgated in school systems.

(Continued)

(Continued)

4. Target setting is an essential component of improvement planning in order to achieve desired outcomes.

5. School systems must spend time working on belief systems. For example, the belief that all children can learn and achieve success, given time and proper supports, must be deeply entrenched in education systems.

6. Learning must become visible and explicit. Students must be able to measure their work, performance, and achievement against clearly established standards.

7. Inequality can manifest itself in many ways if educators are not vigilant. Societies with less inequality have better social outcomes.

8. When students are fully engaged in the learning process, achievement improves.

9. Data are important. Disaggregation of these data is a prerequisite for addressing achievement gaps.

● ● ● ● ACTION STEPS FOR BEING MORE INCLUSIVE AND IMPROVING ACHIEVEMENT

1. Establish and disseminate a rubric of what high expectations look like in a school overall and classrooms specifically.

2. Raise the bar for all students and close achievement gaps.

3. Work with principals to set specific targets, taking into consideration current achievement levels for each school. These improvement targets should be based on growth in student achievement.

4. Address issues of student engagement, well-being, voice, and choice.

5. Disaggregate student achievement data to have a clear picture of who is achieving, what the specific needs are, and what interaction strategies would be most effective.

6. Establish or revitalize parent engagement programs to ensure that they know what is being expected of their children and ways that they can support learning.

7. Develop a system of the capacity building for teachers and principals that can be personalized based on the professional learning needs that they identify.

8. Ensure that there are leading-edge resources that teachers and principals can access anywhere and anytime, such as the following resources developed in Ontario for the capacity building of teachers and principals. These are free for educators and are currently being used by educators around the globe:

What Works?

http://www.edu.gov.on.ca/eng/literacynumeracy/inspire/research/whatWorks.html

Capacity Building Series

http://www.edu.gov.on.ca/eng/literacynumeracy/inspire/research/capacityBuilding.html

The Learning Exchange (formerly LearnTeachLead)

http://thelearningexchange.ca/

5

Holistic Education

Character, Career, the Arts, and Entrepreneurship

CHARACTER DEVELOPMENT

Over the years, I have written extensively about the importance of character development as an essential component of a holistic and comprehensive approach to education.

In an article titled "Character Development: Education at Its Best" (Glaze, 2011), I discussed the purposes of education and concluded that the qualities that make us truly human must be emphasized in schools. They are too important to be left to chance. The fact that schools are in a very special position to develop personal and interpersonal skills, in addition to a strong academic program, puts them in a very strategic role to develop character and citizenship—two areas that are demanding increasing attention. These components of what constitutes a good educator are being recognized across the world as important aspects of democracy building and societal development.

For those who are concerned about the overcrowded curriculum, I hasten to say that character development is not new. It has been described as a way of life—the way we see ourselves and how we behave toward one another. As stated by key character developers such as Marvin Berkowitz, Tom Lickona, and P. Fitch Vincent, students must see what good character looks like and have the opportunity to put these values and behaviors into practice. Berkowitz often says, "Children cannot heed a message they have not heard," and that "a child is the only substance from which a responsible adult can be made" (personal communication).

Character development is fast becoming a worldwide concern. England has been undertaking a renewal of commitment to citizenship development. Other countries have also emphasized character education, describing it as social and emotional learning (United Kingdom) or values, ethics and morals (New South Wales), virtue development and life skills (Lesotho), civics and ethics education (Mexico), values development (Estonia), moral development (Hungary), and personal and social development (Malta), to name a few.

What we do know is that there is renewed interest in providing a more holistic approach to education. Parents are demanding it, business and community members are expecting it, and politicians are seeking avenues to make it happen. It is no longer negotiable that educators improve school cultures and prepare students with the life skills that will help them in their personal lives, in the workplace, and as engaged and concerned citizens. Character development must now become an educational imperative and an outcome of schooling.

I have often used the terms "character education" and "character development" interchangeably. There are subtle differences, but in many cases it boils down to a matter of preference.

When we first proposed and developed this strategy in Ontario, we proposed three components:

- Character development in schools
- Building communities of character
- Character in the workplace

These are briefly described as follows:

1. Character development in schools refers to the process of engaging communities to identify the attributes that would become the major content of the program. Once these attributes are agreed upon by the widest possible cross-section of the community, including business and religious leaders, these attributes are integrated into all programs, policies, practices, and interactions. In most cases, these diverse communities select attributes such as respect, responsibility, honesty, integrity, empathy, fairness, initiative, perseverance, courage, and optimism. The title of the Ontario document *Finding Common Ground: Character Development in Ontario Schools, K–12* clearly expresses the intent of such programs.

2. Building communities of character refers to the process of engaging members of the business and faith communities, government officials, the police, labor, industry, and politicians. Mayors, in particular, and all those who have a vested interest in making communities safe places to live, work, and raise their children, are key to the success of this strategy.

The process for developing communities of character include key action steps, for example:

a. Develop a vision of the community you wish to establish or sustain.

b. Obtain the support of colleagues and key opinion leaders at the local level.

c. Find out what is happening in other jurisdictions. It is not necessary to reinvent the wheel. Look into organizations such as Character First, Character Counts, Character Education Partnership, and other organizations engaged in character education.

d. Establish a local coalition as your Character Council, made up of a diverse group of individuals from every sector of your community (business, education, faith, government, media, etc.) to serve as champions for the initiative. Include "opinion leaders" and individuals who have a great degree of influence within the community.

e. Decide on a name, a logo, and other aspects of your Character Council identity.

f. Combine the visions of your council and your vision into a unified vision of what you would all want your community to be like and to achieve.

g. Develop an action plan that includes key actions, indicators of success, related strategies, timelines, roles, responsibilities, and costs.

h. Delineate and agree on some ground rules and common understandings—including procedures, processes, behaviors, and expected outcomes.

i. Provide character education training for all members of your team.

j. Identify promotional activities, materials, and resources and seek out sponsors to cover costs, if necessary.

k. Organize a special launch of your initiative and provide opportunities for ongoing dialogue.

l. Develop a multipronged communication strategy that expands on two-way communication.

m. Provide activities to engage community members in the process.

n. Meet at least monthly to keep the initiative alive.

o. Provide opportunities for dialogue and involvement of as many community members as possible.

p. Expand your circle of volunteers.

q. Provide opportunities for community members to work cooperatively with their local schools.

r. Evaluate your progress and identify areas requiring future attention.

s. Identify actions to institutionalize the initiative.

t. Agree on strategies to promote sustainability.

3. Character in the workplace: Two of the districts in which I worked, the York Region District School Board and the Kawartha Pine Ridge District School Board (KPR), to the best of my knowledge, were among the first school districts in Canada to develop these character initiatives in a systematic and intentional manner.

In these settings, it became clear that we should not make demands on our communities and schools to engage in character development while those at the central or district office were not modeling what this looks like in action.

As associate and later director of education (chief superintendent), in York Region and KPR, I was fortunate to work with very progressive school board members who wanted to improve their system. None of these character initiatives would have happened without their political support.

There were many examples of people's willingness to think outside the box and to engage in innovative programs to support students and to improve the organizational culture. For example, employees across departments were asked to spend half a day each week working in schools, helping teachers with a variety of tasks, including helping struggling students to read. This was very popular, as all employees had the opportunity to spend time in schools and to see the results of their decision making on the classrooms of the district.

This initiative contributed to the development of a very caring ethos—one that made the workplace a very pleasant place to be. The feedback was very positive. There was a discernible impact on the organizational culture and the service quality that we provided to parents and the community.

The next phase was to engage the business community, ensuring that the character development strategies permeated all organizations and entrenched the key elements in the places where parents and community members convened.

A few years ago, I returned to this community and took my car to the local dealership. As I went up the stairs to the waiting room, there was a sign on the wall that read:

LEXUS: A BUSINESS OF CHARACTER.

ATTRIBUTE OF THE MONTH: OPTIMISM.

This initiative began in the school system. My reflection was that schools do not simply reflect community, as is the pervasive view; schools and districts can shape, lead, and create communities. It is necessary for school leaders to see the role that they can play in community development. Drucker (1999) exhorted leaders to take care of the common good and to become more than leaders in their own organizations. They must lead beyond the walls of their institutions and create the kinds of communities they are proud to leave for their children and grandchildren.

Meaningful community outreach and engagement and forging deeper partnerships and alliances can help school systems reach the heart of leadership.

CAREER DEVELOPMENT

Schools play a pivotal role in the career development of students. We influence their values, attitudes, and career choices. We work collaboratively with parents, community members, and employers to prepare them for the multiple roles that they will have throughout their lives.

We all want our students to become engaged and productive citizens capable of replicating our democracy and making our communities more productive, caring, and engaging. All these purposes include the need to assist students with decision making and other skills necessary to plan and select from the array of options available to them. Schools must also help remove the barriers that truncate the life chances of students and develop a culture of high expectations for learning and achievement. They must promote equitable outcomes, ensuring that factors such as poverty do not determine a child's destiny. Providing equity of outcomes is an imperative that schools must uphold if they are to reach the heart of leadership.

It is important for all those who work with students and their parents to understand the theories of career development and the strategies that work in assisting students navigate the rich array of information that students today have at their disposal.

When working with students, there are numerous issues to consider:

1. The issues related to the career decision making for young women. Although we have come a far way in terms of sex-role ideology and the sex-typing of occupations, one has to be aware that, in some cases, we have fallen behind. These issues must be kept at the forefront of educational thought and practice, as both boys and girls can still be influenced negatively. In my own research, I found that some of the factors that can influence girls' career decision include the following:

   ○ Sex-role ideology

   ○ Role models

   ○ Socioeconomic status

   ○ Family characteristics, such as parental education

   ○ Personal characteristics, such as ethnicity, place of birth, number of years in the country, position in the family, religion, self-knowledge, and exposure to women's studies courses

2. Boys also need systematic programs in career development to ensure that they choose occupations consistent with their interests, aptitudes, needs, and aspirations.

3. Special attention must be given to people from diverse backgrounds and children in special education programs. I am often pleased to see so many young people with special education needs working in supermarkets and other situations. Employers deserve special commendations for the support they have provided to schools to assist in the career development agenda.

For me, career education is an equity issue. We don't want students' career aspirations or expectations to be limited by socioeconomic or other sociocultural factors. Career education has the potential to enhance the roles and life chances of students, and to improve educational outcomes for students in general and particularly for those at risk of dropping out of school or from disadvantaged backgrounds.

Much is being said today about 21st century. This includes social and emotional learning, the development of the "soft skills," grit, resilience, and character. These skills are all essential for, and included in, career development. Teaching these skills requires a cross-curricular, interdisciplinary approach—one that encourages all teachers, regardless of area of specialization, to help students acquire these skills. Teachers, parents, and the community at large have a pivotal role to play in helping students discover their interests, aptitudes, and dispositions and to provide role models and opportunities for students to try out their career interests. Cooperative education, apprenticeship programs, and other work experience initiatives have been very helpful in providing students with a flavor of what the world of work is about.

Throughout our lives, we play many roles. We are students, employees, consumers, citizens, and parents, to name a few. The ability to fulfill these life roles is dependent on education generally and career education specifically. Systematic career education can help shape and enhance our prospects of leading productive, self-sustaining, and satisfying lives. It can rekindle a sense of hope for future success. It has motivated some students to dream and visualize their role and place in society. Through increased self-awareness, students can also recognize that they have the potential to develop the skills necessary to realize their full potential. Ultimately, everyone benefits—the individuals and society as a whole.

THE IMPORTANCE OF THE ARTS IN THE CURRICULUM

A holistic education goes beyond the development of academic skills and helps students live a well-balanced life. This includes, but is not limited to, intellectual curiosity, physical health, emotional well-being, the arts, and positive character. It explicitly connects students to their community, nature, and the broader world around them. And a focus on these areas need not come at the expense of academic achievement. On the contrary, it helps to support it. As documented by Ratey (2008), having students engage in regular physical exercise, for example, helps improve student outcomes in schools. And social and emotional learning has been shown to be as important to student achievement and lifelong learning as more formal academic skills are (Zins, Bloodworth, Weissberg, & Walberg, 2007).

Arts education, which I consider to be as important as the three Rs, is being threatened in many school districts as resources dwindle. This requires our strong advocacy, as we are fully aware of the importance of the arts in the curriculum and in children's lives. More important, we know the vital role that the arts play in our society.

The research is clear. The arts enrich the lives of students and improve test scores. Math, reading, and science marks, abstract reasoning, and spatial skills improve. The literature also points to improvement in self-esteem, self-confidence, cooperation, and self-motivation. It is said that the arts have a positive impact on all areas of the curriculum and, in particular, on creativity.

There is also research on the impact of the arts in terms of music education specifically. One researcher concluded that music education equals brain power. Music lifts our heart and soothes our souls. It is a primary means of communication. Many of our students in bands and plays today will be our orchestra players and actors in the future. We cannot afford to see the disappearance of the arts in our school curriculum. All of us must redouble our efforts to keep these programs alive, because they are woefully underfunded in many jurisdictions.

I will always remember a visit to a school as a new superintendent in one of the school districts in which I worked. The principal would have announced or put in the daily bulletin that I would be visiting the school that day. A student waited alone outside the school until I arrived—long after all the students had gone home. This young man approached me and offered to take me to the music room to show me the state of the instruments. I was saddened to see the taped-up instruments that the students were expected to use. I am not, by any means, blaming anyone. My reason for telling this story is simply to say that so many teachers and principals are working very hard with the scarce resources that they have. We must find new ways to support them and to keep the arts alive.

Visual arts and dance are equally important. They foster multimedia skills through the use of communication, technological, architectural, and other skills that will remain with students throughout their lives.

All students, regardless of background or socioeconomic status, benefit from programs in the arts. We should be particularly vigilant in ensuring that students from poor backgrounds are encouraged and helped to participate in these programs. Musical instruments, for example, are quite expensive. In the face of dwindling resources, we should encourage community members to donate musical instruments to our schools if students living in poor circumstances are to be members of our orchestras and symphonies later on. So often when I am at the theatre, I am preoccupied with the question of how many of the performers come from poor backgrounds. I would guess that there wouldn't be many because of the cost of what they need to participate in these activities. What saddens me most is the unrecognized talent that exists in needy communities and the cultural and societal loss in not nurturing these talents.

The National Governors Association (NGA) Center for Best Practices, in its issue brief (2002), concluded that arts education has an impact on all populations, but most compelling is the advantage provided for at-risk youth. For these students, the arts contribute to increased self-esteem, the acquisition of job skills, and the development of much-needed creative-thinking, problem-solving, and communication skills. The NGA Center for Best Practices asserts that involvement in the arts is one avenue by which at-risk youth can acquire the various competencies necessary to become economically self-sufficient over the long term.

It is primarily through the avenue of public schools that students who live in poverty will ever have the opportunity to learn a musical instrument or to participate in an arts program. I have long concluded that there is an equity imperative inherent in arts education.

The many benefits of education in the arts are well documented. One study found that children who study the arts are:

- Four times more likely to be recognized for academic achievement
- Elected to class office within their schools three times as often
- Four times more likely to participate in math and science fairs
- Three times more likely to win an award for school attendance
- Four times more likely to win an award for writing an essay or a poem

Key competencies of cognitive growth that are developed through an education in the arts include

- Perception of relationships
- Skill in finding multiple solutions to problems
- Attendance to nuance
- Adaptability
- Decision-making skills
- Visualization of goals and outcomes

These research findings leave no doubt in our minds that arts education represents education at its best. For that reason, we must continue to make a compelling case for the incorporation of the arts in the curriculum—providing students with the skills they need to be productive participants in society.

THE ENTREPRENEURIAL SPIRIT AND MIND-SET

Educators today continue to work at developing a holistic approach to teaching and learning. They will assert that they educate hearts as well as minds. They teach students to be critical thinkers, problem solvers, and solution finders. They develop global perspectives, good character, and strong intra- and interpersonal competencies. They continue to emphasize academic achievement and well-being, preparing students for postsecondary education and the workplace, and to become responsible and engaged citizens.

With youth unemployment being a major concern today, there is a need to position entrepreneurship not just as a business skill but as a life skill as we prepare students to find innovative solutions to the problems that they will inevitably confront. This combination of skills encourages an individual to turn ideas into action. It enables innovative improvements, solves complex problems, creates social value, and builds prosperity.

Zhao (2012) addresses these issues. He mentions three types of entrepreneurs, with the caveat that entrepreneurs are not simply those who start a business in order to maximize profits. There are *social entrepreneurs* who apply entrepreneurial principles to achieve social change, there are *intrapreneurs* who make significant innovations within the organizations in which they work, and there are also *policy entrepreneurs* who make noteworthy policy improvements within public and government institutions.

What is positive about this multipronged approach to turning ideas into action is that all students, regardless of their career orientation or the career clusters that they choose to pursue, have the potential to be entrepreneurial. But, first, we must try to address some of the criticisms leveled at us in the field of education.

One such criticism is that we stifle curiosity and creativity. As educators, in the spirit of reflection and introspection discussed earlier in this book, we must ask ourselves a critical question: Do we, indeed, stifle curiosity and creativity? I think we should take this criticism quite seriously. Defensiveness is not helpful. We must improve. These issues and concerns are too important for the future of our students.

Zhao states that the longer students are in school, the less curious they become. Also, high school students who exhibit creative personalities are more likely to drop out of school than their less creative counterparts are. Knowing what we now know about the unpredictable nature of the future of work in traditional occupations, we need to do more to foster the entrepreneurial mind-set in all our schools to ensure that our students will be able to deal with occupational, workplace, and career uncertainty. This important aspect of education should not be left to chance. We all need to practice what we preach about developing the entrepreneurial spirit in our schools.

We do know that parents and the community have a role to play as well. Schools cannot do this alone. But ours is an opportunity not to be missed. Zhao would argue that qualities such as creativity, curiosity, imagination, initiative, intelligent risk taking, collaboration, opportunity recognition, self-confidence, and strong people skills must be developed in schools. There is consensus that a well-prepared citizen of the future has to be creative, entrepreneurial, and globally competent.

Many also agree that human beings are born with the desire and potential to create and innovate, to dream and imagine, and to challenge and improve the status quo. But this potential, according to Zhao, can be either suppressed or amplified, based on our experiences.

Some governments have already instituted entrepreneurial studies as an important part of the curriculum. Many teachers have been working hard to implement programs that contribute to these goals. Project-based learning and cooperative education programs, for example, provide avenues and opportunities that support the development of the entrepreneurial spirit and mind-set.

In order for us to achieve this goal, it is important for us to continue to support organizations such as The Learning Partnership in Ontario, as well as the schools that already have established programs in their efforts to work with business, labor, and industry to further embed the qualities necessary for entrepreneurship to thrive.

A STRONG COMMITMENT
TO ADVOCACY

In education, being an effective leader involves advocating successfully on behalf of the students and communities we serve. In this way, effective leaders speak out and take action in order to overcome resistance and affect change. They raise awareness of issues, build coalitions, and influence policy. Kendrick (2008) outlines several advocacy functions that are at times required of effective leaders. These include

- Bringing attention to crucial issues affecting devalued and disadvantaged people
- Creating occasions that make people think and reconsider
- Offering a vision of what could be better
- Being willing to take seriously views discounted by the authorities or majorities
- Seeking to gain movement and increase pressure on issues that are stalled
- Forcing into play questions of right and wrong in terms of how people are treated
- Creating a sense of hope and affirmation for people who are struggling against and suffering because of oppression

Glaze et al. (2012) proposed twelve key attributes of advocates. We stated that the ability to influence others is a skill that all leaders today must possess. We recognized that there are often inherent risks and obstacles to be overcome. We identified a few insights into the role of advocates in education today, with the recommendation that advocacy is a strong requirement of all those who aspire to leadership positions. It goes with the job. This means that advocates take on issues that are often unpopular and that go against the prevailing views of those in positions of power and influence. Advocates are often strong and resolute in their conviction that something must be done to remedy the situation for the benefit of others. They seek to understand, deconstruct, and confront issues such as power and power relationships, recognizing that these are often roadblocks to organizational effectiveness. Most important, they engage in courageous conversations. The topics that they address are often not popular. In fact, taking on some of these issues can be seen as career limiting. But, nonetheless, they seek to influence attitudes and decisions to support children and their learning and achievement and issues that are important to staff and community.

Advocates recognize the characteristics of equitable and inclusive schools. They are passionate about issues related to student engagement, student voice, and choice. The centrality of students in all that the school does and stands for must be defended. Schools exist because of students.

Advocates believe in developing strong communities. They are also vociferous in their assertion that schools should not simply reflect communities; they must challenge, change, and create the communities they want.

Advocacy today means believing that schools must serve the needs of *all* children, especially those who are disadvantaged. House and Martin (1998) state that a social advocacy approach is based on the belief that individual and collective action must be taken to right injustices or to improve conditions for the benefit of an individual or group.

I remember that early in my leadership career, I did take on a few issues that were considered controversial. One revolved around fighting to keep pregnant girls in school and another had to do with initiating a program for expelled students. These issues were described as controversial at the time. Many thought that by becoming an advocate for these unpopular issues, I would truncate my career trajectory. But at the time, my only concern was for the welfare of these students, who were, for the most part, children from working-class backgrounds. In my experience, all schools must have teachers and administrators who see themselves as advocates for children from challenging circumstances. If there is no one in the school to be the advocate for these students, they may not be motivated to remain in school and to receive their high school diploma. I have always felt that, under my watch as an educational leader, "there will be no throwaway kids."

It is my conviction that there should be a group in every school that is championing the cause of equity, diversity, social justice, and inclusivity. This group of committed individuals works with near-evangelical zeal to remove barriers and roadblocks. They are willing to take risks to support needy children, many of whom do not have advocates of their own.

WORKING WITH DIVERSITY: COMMUNITY OUTREACH, ENGAGEMENT, AND DEVELOPMENT

Diversity, equity, and effective leadership form a "necessary nexus," especially in education, where equity is considered "a prerequisite of educational excellence" (McCarthy & Webb, 1990, p. 10). This type of equitable leadership involves respecting the rights of all those affected by a leader's actions (Gini, 1998). In schools, this becomes particularly salient, as we know that certain groups— particularly females, visible minorities, and students and teacher educators who identify as members of the lesbian, gay, bisexual, transgender (LGBT) community—often experience various forms of harassment in schools (Datnow, 1998; Lugg, 2003; Orenstein, 2002; Stein, 2002). It is important to know that in many settings, a Q has been added to include those who identify themselves as queer—that is, LGBTQ. Inclusive leadership is thus concerned with bringing about social justice, by meaningfully including all people in institutional practices and processes (Ryan, 2006). It involves assessing who is currently excluded from resources and decision making and taking steps to change this. In this view, achieving social justice ultimately occurs "when changes to the system allow for meaningful inclusion of everyone, particularly those who are consistently disadvantaged or marginalized" (Ryan, 2006, p. 6).

Throughout my career, I have seen the need to be inclusive in addressing what I refer to as human rights issues, long accepting the fact that if we say we believe in human rights, we cannot be selective about the human beings for whom we will advocate. It is an all-or-none proposition.

In addition, in my most introspective moments, I ask myself: How can I as a black, immigrant, female—I could go on and on defining other aspects of who I am—discriminate against others? How can I, being aware of what discrimination looks like and feels like, engage in the behaviors that I have spent my life trying to eradicate? How can I as a leader, erect structures and approve of policies and processes similar to the ones that I have tried hard to dismantle? How can I engage in interactions that do not fully acknowledge and respect the humanity that I have demanded we see in others?

Will I instead use the little power and influence that I have to advance the cause of those who experience victimization, marginalization, or exclusion? The answer has to be a resounding yes! I can hear my grandmother's voice saying something like, "Much is expected from those who have been given much." Those early teachings have stayed with me throughout my life.

Reaching the heart of leadership also requires community outreach, engagement, and development. This involves a concern for the broader community (Kalshoven, Den Hartog, & De Hoogh, 2011). This includes the people and places that schools serve, as well as issues of sustainability. Indeed, it has been argued that real school improvement requires that schools themselves be transformed from organizations to communities (Sergiovanni, 1992). Furthermore, it should be noted that in order for ethical leadership to be truly practiced in schools, the broader school community must be involved (Strike, 2007).

This is also about "leading beyond the walls," to use the words of Peter Drucker (1999), who said,

> Society in all developed countries has become pluralist and is becoming more pluralist day by day. . . . But all early pluralist societies destroyed themselves because no one took care of the common good. . . . If our modern pluralist society is to escape the same fate, the leaders of all institutions will have to learn to be leaders beyond the walls. They will have to learn that it is not enough for them to lead their own institutions, though that is their first requirement. They will have to learn to become leaders in the community. In fact, they will have to learn to create community. (p. 9)

Reaching the heart of leadership means that leaders must expand their reach, moving beyond the walls of their schools and district offices to reach into the community. As Drucker says, school leaders should not only reflect community; they should seek to create community. By expanding their sphere of influence, they will harness the energy and vitality of community members to find common ground in order to reach their goals.

A case in point is how we worked with the largest possible cross-section of community members in the York Region District School Board, as well as in the Kawartha Pine Ridge District School Board in Ontario a few years later, to initiate character development programs that represented attributes chosen by the community. Examples of the actions taken under this initiative are described earlier in the chapter. Suffice it to say that they are examples of how school leaders can work collaboratively with the community to take everyone to a new level of understanding and functioning. Community and municipal leaders are among those who point to the differences these programs make in community development and cohesion.

Leadership Lessons Learned

1. Character and citizenship development has become an educational imperative.

2. Parents and politicians across the globe are identifying character development as an important aspect of education in general, and democracy building and citizenship development in particular.

3. There is a renewed interest in holistic education, as many think that the pendulum has swung too far on the student achievement agenda.

4. Regardless of religious affiliation, we can find common ground on the universal values we hold in common.

5. In order to address issues that can be very divisive, it is important to engage the widest possible local coalition of community members to grapple with each issue and to arrive at consensus.

6. Politicians, parents, and other key decision makers must be involved in the process of implementing any aspect of education that is based on values and personal attributes.

7. Including the business community and student leaders contributes significantly to the success of the character development initiative.

8. Character development significantly changes the culture, ethos, and climate of a school district, which, in turn, improves student achievement.

9. Student achievement improves with the implementation of character education. Teachers say they are able to spend more time teaching and less time on discipline.

10. Schools do not have to simply reflect society and societal values; they can also shape society.

11. The education of specific populations—including girls, boys, and immigrants, to name a few—is not a not a *fait accompli*. Despite decades of attention, many groups remain behind as some systems still struggle to close achievement gaps.

12. There should be no "throw-away kids." We need all students in our schools today to receive a good education so that they can be contributing members of our society.

13. A social justice approach is about inclusion of those who are disadvantaged or marginalized.

14. Adopting a human rights approach means that we are inclusive of everyone. As educators, we cannot say we believe in human rights if we are selective of the human beings for whom we will advocate.

15. Effective leadership means "leading beyond the walls" of organizations in order to create community.

● ● ● ● ACTION STEPS TO ENHANCE STUDENT SUCCESS

1. Initiate programs that foster improvement in human relationships and attitudes toward others.

2. Put in place systematic career development programs for specific groups—for example, boys, children who live in poverty,

(Continued)

(Continued)

or any group that is not achieving to the maximum of its potential.

3. Target children with special education for career education to enable them to be self-sustaining members of society, whenever possible.

4. Ensure that students see the relationship between learning and earning—between what they are learning in school and requirements in the world of work.

5. Integrate experiential learning into all academic programs.

6. Provide the strongest possible advocacy to ensure that the arts remain an integral part of educational programs.

7. Develop programs that foster the entrepreneurial spirit, creativity, and the development of innovative solutions to the problems that students will encounter.

8. Discuss and recommend strategies to address the serious criticisms leveled at those of us who serve in education by Zhao in his book *World Class Learners* (2012) that

   a. We stifle creativity and curiosity.

   b. The longer students stay in school, the less curious they become.

   c. High school students who exhibit creative personalities are more likely to drop out of school than their less creative counterparts are.

9. Ensure that project-based learning, cooperative education, and entrepreneurial skills development are an integral part of the school curriculum.

10. Examine equity policies, programs, and practices to ensure that they have specific and measurable strategies to realize their promise of educating all students successfully, especially those who are marginalized.

6

Capacity Building for System, School, and Professional Improvement

Regardless of how well an organization is currently performing, effective leaders continually seek out ways to do things better. Today's imperative for leaders is continuous improvement. In education specifically, contrary to popular belief, it is now recognized that schools do not fundamentally improve because of the introduction of a particular new policy or program, or changes to the organizational structure (Anderson & Kumari, 2009). Rather, real improvement occurs when schools become learning organizations that continually monitor actions, progress, and results, and then make changes accordingly so that a shared vision can be achieved (Copeland, 2003; Fullan, 2005; Hawley & Sykes, 2007). In this view, change is something that occurs continuously and as a result of specific actions.

It is essential that leaders focus on strategies to build a culture of collaborating on continuous improvement. It is now commonly accepted that schools can do this through engaging in more collective efforts, such as developing professional learning communities (DuFour, Eaker, & DuFour, 2005; Thiessen & Anderson, 1999). And we do know that if schools, districts, and other organizations are to realize continuous improvement, they must be willing to invest in, support, and develop their people. Even in times of dwindling resources, funding and other resources for capacity building must remain a priority.

CAPACITY BUILDING: THE ESSENCE OF DISTRICT AND SCHOOL IMPROVEMENT

In *High School Graduation, K–12 Strategies That Work*, Glaze, Mattingley, and Andrews (2013) discuss the pivotal role that capacity building plays in improvement efforts. We asserted that one of the keys to improvement in Ontario in the last ten years has been the fact that Ontario, contrary to many jurisdictions, chose capacity building as is primary improvement tool. First of all, our team identified and provided supports to address the wide range of professional learning opportunities that existed for educators, recognizing how needs varied with individuals and across the diverse province. These included direct training, leadership development programs, webcasts by leading international experts, research monographs written by university professors and staff, multiple print resources, a Schools on the Move initiative to share promising practices (especially from schools in challenging circumstances), networking opportunities, coaching, and summer institutes for teachers.

We paid attention to the research that shows that classroom instruction and school leadership have the most profound impact on student achievement. People may have the will, but they need to develop the skills to improve student learning. As well, Reeves (2009) points out,

> Of all the variables that influence student achievement, the two that have the most profound influence are teacher quality and leadership quality. (p. 60)

Reeves (2016) also provides new insights and strategies that leaders can use for continuous improvement. Although there is no doubt that socioeconomic factors influence student results, the preponderance of the evidence suggests that teachers and leaders make a profound difference in the lives of the students they serve.

This means that districts that truly want to improve outcomes for all students must build capacity in their teachers and leaders. As educators, we need to seek opportunities to learn together. Traditionally, teaching has been a very isolated profession, even though we have known for a long time that the research that indicates that the best learning occurs in collaboration with others and that teachers' skills, knowledge, beliefs, and understandings are key factors in improving the achievement of all students.

The report *Unlocking Potential for Learning*, by Campbell, Fullan, and Glaze (2006), presented research to determine the strategies that were being used in the districts that were most successful. This report identified twelve key components of effective practice, linked to four broad strategic areas:

1. Leading with purpose and focusing direction
2. Designing a coherent strategy; coordinating implementation and reviewing outcomes
3. Developing precision in knowledge, skills, and daily practices for improving learning
4. Sharing responsibility through building partnerships

This research, described in *High School Graduation* (Glaze et al. 2013), was shared across the province. Districts therefore began to network with "like districts" to share promising practices, build capacity, and learn from one another.

McKinsey and Company (2009) state that the world's best performing systems share similar characteristics. They

- Focus on ensuring that students receive the *best possible instruction*
- Hire the best people possible

- *Ensure that capacity building* is a priority (i.e., develop their people)
  - They include job-embedded professional learning
  - They pay attention to the professionalization of teachers
- Establish a sound *foundation in literacy and numeracy*
- Focus on ensuring *excellence in teaching and school leadership*
- Set minimum proficiency *targets* that are *ambitious and achievable*
- *Provide the resources* required to achieve priorities
- Ensure *transparency and accountability* for student achievement results, with the effective use of data to inform instructional decisions
- Use a *range of assessments* within the school and district as well as external assessments (e.g., international assessments to determine international comparability)
- Provide a *rigorous and relevant curriculum*, defining what students should know, understand, and are able to do, and create the accompanying teaching content

We have also learned many lessons from Finland. Sahlberg (2011) tells us that building networks among schools that stimulate and spread innovation helps explain Finland's success in making "strong school performance a consistent and predictable outcome throughout the education system with less than 5% variation in student performance between schools" (p. 40).

What we do know, therefore, is that the systems across the world that are demonstrating continuous improvement without demoralizing or alienating their teachers are the ones that have consciously decided to base their improvement strategies on what research says. They have eschewed the more draconian measures often wrapped in the cloak of accountability to focus on what is effective, while maintaining the morale of those who are expected to do the work. I am convinced that if people knew what to do to improve learning and achievement, they would have done it. If they are not doing this to get the results we all want, they need professional development in order to be able to deliver on the expectations. Hence, my conclusion is that capacity building has to be the essence of all improvement efforts.

IMPROVING ONTARIO SCHOOLS: A STRATEGY THAT WORKS

Capacity building is certainly the hallmark that ensures success and improvement. This has been recognized by leaders such as Schleicher and Stewart, who in 2008 said,

> Perhaps the most important lesson we can learn from international comparisons is that strong performance and improvement are always possible. Countries such as Japan, Korea, Finland and Canada display strong overall performance and, equally important, show that a disadvantaged socioeconomic background does not necessarily result in poor performance at school.

In addition, in a discussion on how Ontario harnesses the skills of tomorrow, the OECD wrote the following in 2011:

> Not only do Canadian students perform well in PISA, they do so despite their socio-economic status, first language or whether they are native Canadians or recent immigrants. Canada has achieved success within a highly federated system that accommodates a diverse student population. This study examines Canada's success through an in-depth look at the education system of the country's largest province, Ontario. It describes how the province combines a demand for excellence with extensive capacity-building, and fosters a climate of trust and mutual respect among all stakeholders.

Educators and policy makers from across the globe have been visiting Ontario to learn about the strategies that continue to make a difference. I have personally arranged educational tours for visitors from many countries. The topics that they are most interested in all revolve around educational reform and the actions that make a difference. But some of the most frequently requested topics are how we have developed our leaders, how we have built capacity at all levels of the system, the strategies we have implemented to narrow achievement gaps, and what it takes to achieve both excellence and equity.

As I reflect upon our journey, I recall that in the early years of the improvement strategy, we went through several phases of implementation:

- Developing consensus
- Building capacity
- Implementing effective high-impact strategies
- Intensifying our efforts
- Sharpening our focus
- Consolidating our emphasis
- Requiring deeper implementation
- Renewing our commitments

There was a need to review constantly what we were doing in order to ensure that we were on the right track. The focus on capacity building at all levels of the system, along with providing the resources that teachers and principals needed, was the hallmark of that improvement strategy. It is important for me to comment on the issue of resources, as this is often used as an excuse for nonperformance or lack of improvement. Ontario did not have an abundance of resources. This strategy took place at a time when resources were dwindling. Surely, improving systems requires resources—human, financial, and material. But I am convinced that *will* and *skill* are more salient variables than financial resources are in school improvement. From my experience, if employees have the knowledge and skills to implement the agenda, they will be less cynical and more motivated to do the work that is necessary to achieve the desired results.

One of the lessons we learned is that in bringing about large-scale systemic reform, characterized engagement, commitment, ownership, and sustainability, certain actions had to be taken.

● ● ● ● STRATEGIES
FOR CAPACITY BUILDING
AND SYSTEM IMPROVEMENT

From a system perspective, we worked collaboratively to

- Instill a sense of urgency
- Foster a spirit of mutual trust, respect, and collegiality
- Engage partners within and outside of the system, including faculties of education and university professors
- Focus on improving both excellence and equity
- Build a strong research orientation, with an emphasis on *what works*
- Reject the "shame and blame" philosophy
- Eschew the "one-size-fits- all" syndrome
- Establish a small number of precise goals
- Include strong character development programs and other programs that address behaviors
- Provide positive pressure and support
- Base improvement strategies on current research
- Develop partnerships with other agencies to support learning
- Establish clear expectations
- Provide necessary resources
- Target supports to meet specific groups and unique needs
- Invest in people by building capacity
- Share promising practices
- Implement strategies to monitor progress regularly
- Stay the course
- Celebrate successes
- Take stock and measure progress, and make corrections if necessary

At the classroom level, it was necessary to

- Set high expectations for all students

(Continued)

(Continued)

- Build on student interest, backgrounds, and strengths
- Encourage student voice and choice
- Provide tasks that demand higher-order thinking
- Differentiate instruction
- Make learning intentions and success criteria clear to students
- Help students set learning goals
- Use formative and summative assessments
- Teach literacy across all subject areas
- Scaffold and chunk instruction
- Provide students with examples of "good" work
- Provide opportunities for purposeful talk
- Focus on nonfiction writing for multiple purposes
- Use word walls and anchor charts to support instruction
- Provide a diverse classroom library
- Make learning experiences practical and relevant
- Ensure that classroom materials reflect the diversity of the class

At the provincial level, it was necessary to

- Establish a vision for excellence and equity
- Communicate the expectation of continuous improvement
- Reinforce continually that all students can achieve and that all teachers can teach at a high level
- Lead with purpose and focus district direction
- Prioritize resources
- Invest in leadership development and teacher professional learning—any time, any place
- Provide opportunities for professional learning
- Differentiate supports
- Provide alignment and coherence

- Develop inclusive curriculum, instruction, and interventions to improve teaching and learning for all students

- Establish strategies for system and school-level monitoring, review, feedback, and accountability

- Ask directors, superintendents, and curriculum experts to visit schools to monitor progress and provide support

---

It is also important to build capacity to help all leaders understand the needs, aspirations, and expectations of students today. It is easy to forget the societal changes that make life so difficult for the children in our care. All educators should be sensitized to the challenges facing our students today. These include the following:

● ● ● ● CHALLENGES FACING OUR STUDENTS

- A search for meaning and purpose
- Realizing a sense of belonging
- Negative peer group influences
- Cultural clashes and generational conflicts
- Developing the competencies and attributes needed to enter a changing workplace
- Feelings of alienation and marginalization
- Bullying and other school safety issues
- Bombardment of negative media images
- Environmental issues and threats, such as global warming
- Racism, sexism, homophobia, and classism, among other "isms"
- Families in crisis
- Mental health issues
- An aging population, with the concern that students will have to work twice as hard to pay the pensions of the large cohort of baby boomers

At the same time, this long list of negative factors belies the fact that young people today have many options and opportunities—some of which we never had when we were growing up. While recognizing their challenges, we must also acknowledge and help them seize the numerous opportunities that are open to them. Some of these are as follows:

● ● ● ● OPTIONS AND OPPORTUNITIES THAT OUR STUDENTS BENEFIT FROM

- Diverse forums in which students can develop personal and interpersonal qualities, such as empathy, respect, and understanding of others
- The ability to build positive relationships across lines of societal demarcations
- Supports to develop a sense of individuality, inner strength, and character
- Global prospects for career and humanitarian pursuits
- Opportunities to engage with more diverse groups of people, which increases learning about cultural similarities, values, differences, and needs
- Extended opportunities for networking through technology
- Multiple options to try out a wide spectrum of occupations and career pathways
- Opportunities to practice what true inclusion means and to relate to students with special education needs
- Opportunities for community engagements to help build peaceful and caring communities
- Learning from a wealth of information from a variety of sources to help students become critical and discerning consumers and users of knowledge
- Opportunities to develop resilience
- Forums to hone skills, creativity, and innovation
- Experiences that develop an entrepreneurial spirit

- Strategies to learn what it means to be politically active and to be advocates for the rights and needs of others, social justice, and more equitable societies

- Learning from elders what it means to be stewards of a promising future

- The need to embrace science and technology, including new efforts to institutionalize STEM (science, technology, engineering, and math) innovations and to find creative options and resolutions to address current societal challenges

- Developing the knowledge, attitudes, skills, and dispositions to become global leaders and solution finders who think critically and analytically; feeling deeply and empathetically and to act wisely and ethically

---

At the same time, it is important for us to listen to our youth. It is easy to think that because of their lack of experience, they may not know the perils and pitfalls that lie ahead. If we are sensitive to their needs, feelings, and aspirations, we will hear their cries for understanding, support, and opportunities to try your new experiences.

Some young people are shy—others have fragile egos. They must be protected. We only have to think of how easily we are hurt by negative comments or underestimation of our ability or potential.

But I hasten to say how much more careful teachers and principals are today about how children are treated. I have really seen improvements in recent years. I have visited schools in which children hang onto the principal as she walks the halls. In one school I visited, as I walked the hall with the principal, many students ran up to her and hugged her. One child started crying and later told the principal that her parents were fighting a lot and that they were on the verge of a separation. Children sense caring and empathy in their teachers and principals.

I also know of principals who have changed their school culture in dramatic ways in a short period of time. In one school, a principal told me that in the past, as she walked the halls, the students would run up to her to show her their toys or some other artifacts they had brought from home. But she knew she had changed the culture when one child, from a poor background, came up to her and instead of showing her a toy, she showed her a page of her writing!

What might some of the specific needs of our children be? How are they being expressed? Examples are as follows:

How do students express their needs?

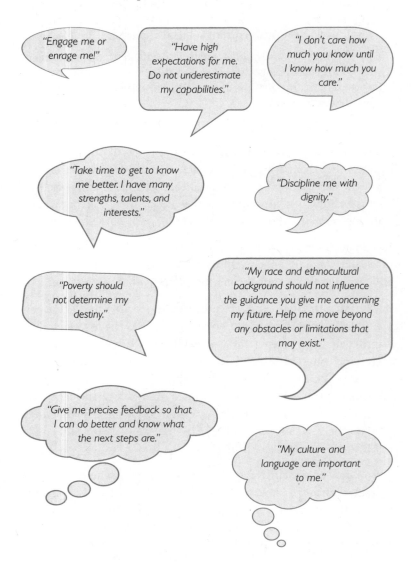

"Please don't tell me not to speak my home language at school. I want to continue to be multilingual."

"I will do my part. You must provide me with a guarantee that I will be a literate graduate."

"The three Rs are important to me. But I also want to be a person of character."

"Help me become a world-class citizen with 21st century skills."

"Career development is essential for my future. I want to know the relationship between learning and earning."

"Help me develop character. It is said that character is destiny."

"I don't want to become a school dropout. Help me graduate."

"I want to be resilient—to be able to cope with life's challenges. Help me!"

"Attendance is important. If I am not at school, I cannot learn. But I find school so boring!"

"My parents may not show up for meetings. But they care about my future. They trust the school to do the best for me. That is how it was in their old country."

One of the experiences that will remain with me forever is when I was one of five commissioners on Ontario's Royal Commission on Learning.

After we conducted our hearings, it was clear that the voices and perspectives of diverse groups, immigrant populations, and individuals who live in poverty, among others, were not represented. After all, many of these individuals, some of whom did not have positive experiences in school, would not show up to present papers at hearings. So we asked for more time to do a special outreach to marginalized communities to get their perspective. I chose to set up a booth in the largest mall in the area and to engage people in the discussion. But the experience I will always remember is when I visited a detention center for young offenders.

There were about twenty young male offenders in the room, ages seventeen to eighteen. There was an equal number of guards. I asked them questions about their schooling. These young men were open, articulate, and forthright. A young aboriginal man asked, with great sadness and anger in his voice, "Do you know what it is like to go through school and see, in all the books you have to read, your people presented as savages?" A young black man piped up, "Do you have any idea how it hurts to see your people always presented in a negative light?" He continued, "In all my years in school, I have never seen a positive black role model in the book I had to read. This affects you!"

What was interesting to me—and somewhat painful—was that all these young men talked about the curriculum, what it left out, and how it affected them.

Leadership Lessons Learned

1. When I worked in New Zealand some years ago, I noticed that one of the tenets of their curriculum was the following: "The curriculum should not alienate the student." I thought that this was a profound statement. Students will not learn if they are not able to connect with the content of what they are learning, at best. At worst, they will

"refuse to learn," to use the statement of another researcher, because of the dissonance that this approach creates.

2. Ensuring instructional effectiveness and developing leadership are the most important variables in improving student learning and achievement.

3. School districts must ensure that there is an adequate budget to support professional learning. Too often these programs are the first on the chopping block. Investing in people is the surest means of creating a successful organization.

4. Target setting at the system, school, and classroom levels should no longer be seen as part of the right-wing conservative agenda. It is an essential ingredient to measure impact and outcomes.

5. We will not be successful in our reform efforts if we do not take time to build consensus, encourage buy-in, and promote goodwill and remove the distractors that stand in the way of progress.

6. Improvement requires a high degree of coherence at all levels of the school system.

7. As educators, we should closely listen to the student stories and statements about adult behavior. Some students do have negative experiences in school. We cannot fail in our ability to protect them fully—physically and psychologically.

● ● ● ● ACTION STEPS FOR DISTRICT AND SCHOOL IMPROVEMENT

1. Evaluate your system performance against the standards established by McKinsey and Company (2009) regarding the world's best performing systems.

2. We all look longingly at the Finnish education system regarding their high levels of teacher qualification, the importance of capacity building, and the establishment of networks without demoralizing or alienating their teachers. Learn about the systems that are on an upward trajectory without the casualties often associated with school reform.

(Continued)

(Continued)

3. Study the strategies being used in schools in challenging circumstances that are achieving beyond expectations, build a network of those schools, include a few principals of schools in similar circumstances that are doing well, identify a few areas of focus, and meet regularly to support people in turning around those schools.

4. Include teacher unions in a joint, targeted approach to provide exchange programs within and between schools and districts to facilitate teacher professional learning.

5. Provide opportunities for meaningful student involvement in school activities. Ensure that all students are engaged in some form of extracurricular activity.

6. Provide leadership development for students, especially those who feel alienated or marginalized.

7. Conduct a study to find out the reasons that some students do not complete their high school education. Use the data to provide the programs that they say would have made a difference to their sense of connection with school.

8. Ensure that every school has a mentorship program to enable students to develop a supportive relationship with a significant adult.

7

Achieving Results, Determining Impact, Recognizing Responsibilities

ACHIEVING RESULTS

Effective leadership involves a range of activities, including creating a mission, setting strategy, motivating others, and building a positive culture. But as stated by Goleman (2000), "the leader's singular job is to get results" (p. 78). And this is as true in education as in any other field.

However, it is only through a continued focus on outcomes and results that any leader can tell whether his or her efforts are the right ones, and can make adjustments accordingly. Ulrich, Zenger, and Smallwood (1999) outline a series of steps that leaders can take to become more results focused. Ulrich suggests that the focus should be on results, clear communication of targets and expectations, and using the personal and social resources that the members bring to the group. He recommends experimentation and innovation and the pursuit of new ways of enhancing performance. For him, seeking feedback from others to facilitate improvement is expected of leaders.

The actions proposed by Ulrich and his colleagues reflect some of the key imperatives for achieving desired outcomes in any organization. These include focus, taking responsibility, communicating clearly, utilizing talent and building capacity, innovating, and seeking feedback. The actions include reliance on the team and providing motivation for continuous improvement of outcomes.

DETERMINING IMPACT

It is important for leaders to spend time reflecting on their careers in education. It is a quest to determine the impact they have had on people and organizations. Leaders engage in reflection, asking whether they made good decisions, whether they advanced the goals of their province or state and the organizations for which they worked, and, most important, whether they treated people with the dignity and respect that are consistent with their values and beliefs. It is a questioning of whether or not they reached the heart of leadership.

Some leaders do seek out feedback. But we do know that the higher up we go in organizations, the less likely it is for people to provide us with open, honest feedback. But leaders must make an effort to solicit comments from people so that they can assess the impact they are having on others' work. It also means that leaders should not expect gratitude or validation. It is a pleasure when this happens, but it should not be a *quid pro quo* of leadership.

John Hattie's Visible Learning research (2009) has provided definitive findings for educators on what works best in education. We no longer have to guess about what constitutes effective practices. Hattie has helped educators shift the focus in education *away* from initiatives and mandates and *toward* creating assessment-capable, high-achieving learners. This framework is the most expansive, powerful, proven, and unprecedented educational research base in the world, empowering educators to examine *evidence*, take *action*, create an *impact*, and *change the narrative* of modern education.

Individuals who attend Hattie's training sessions, conferences, and workshops have an opportunity to focus on the *evidence* base of Hattie and other thought leaders, along with the *actions* of teachers around the world; to understand the *impact* that educators are having on student outcomes; and to learn from the experiences of educators around the world who have put Visible Learning methods into practice. These sessions, which I have had the pleasure of experiencing, help educators understand the school and classroom factors that most influence student performance. They also help educators learn about the latest learning innovations and ground-breaking research on what works best in improving student achievement, along with strategies for transforming student outcomes through instructional leadership, identifying and monitoring learning intentions, and overcoming the challenges and barriers to creating Visible Learning schools. Finally, these sessions allow educators to become part of the global education network that is changing the way we think and talk about teaching and learning in the 21st century.

In reflecting on our careers, one focus has to be on the impact we have had on people and how their lives have been affected. Reaching the heart of leadership is not about fulfilling personal ambitions, nor about pursuing well-crafted agendas. It is ultimately about service—to others and to our society.

In describing this philosophy, we must consider the fundamental questions that Robert Greenleaf (1977) asked. He used the term "servant leadership" in the 1970s, when I did my initial postgraduate studies and began to look critically into the practice of leadership. The takeaway for leaders has to be the question of who benefits from our leadership. Greenleaf also challenged us to make sure that no one is further disadvantaged as a result of our leadership; instead, people should continue to be further enhanced and continue to grow as individuals and professionals.

RECOGNIZING RESPONSIBILITIES

Still another focus of *Reaching the Heart of Leadership* is to recognize our responsibilities and privileges. One way to do this is to recognize what the privilege of professionalism entails. One of the lessons I have learned—and, indeed, one of my conclusions I have arrived at—is that leadership is a privilege, a responsibility, and a moral imperative. And particularly when there is unequal distribution of power, as discussed earlier, the relationship does become a moral one. That moral imperative helps us treat people as we want to be treated, and to ensure that the best of who we are as human beings comes to the fore in the workplace and all other settings in which we are seen as leaders with influence.

My ultimate conclusion is that leadership is a privilege—a privilege of professionalism. The person who said this best, to my mind, was Albert Shanker, the legendary president of the Federation of Teachers in the United States. He said:

> We do not have the right to be called professionals and we will never convince the public that we are unless we are prepared honestly to decide what constitutes competence and incompetence in our profession and apply those definitions to ourselves and to our colleagues. (1985)

I have also spent a lot of time over the course of my career to reflect on the characteristics of a profession. Three points are worth mentioning if, as professionals, we are to reach the heart of leadership. These include the issue of high standards, the balance of professional autonomy with accountability, and the fact that members must be seen as acting in the interest of their "clients."

High standards means that we uphold the highest ideals of our profession and constantly strive to raise the bar of performance and achievement for ourselves and others. Balancing professional autonomy with accountability is also very important, especially during these times of an increased call for greater responsibility from parents, politicians, and other stakeholders. One is reminded of Fullan's (1989) exhortation that there is no such thing as isolated autonomy. As public servants, we cannot close our doors and do our own thing. We must always be open to criticism and scrutiny and must be prepared to listen and improve. After all, one of the stages in the development of a profession is that there is increasing demand and public expectation for quality in the services provided. If we say we believe in continuous improvement, we should welcome this challenge, recognizing that arrogance and indifference to input and feedback are anathema to the kind of responsiveness that is required of public "servants" today.

Acting in the interest of the client is one of the most important tenets of one's professionalism. It represents fidelity to the sacred bond we forge in our relationship with people if we are to be worthy of their trust and confidence in our skills, intentions, and actions. It requires being nonjudgmental, while at the same time being willing to point out and confront the behaviors that may thwart the goals you have jointly identified. It also means that the needs of individuals must be preeminent, superseding all other interests.

When teachers and principals act in the interest of their "clients," it means that they put the children first. In this regard, I am reminded of the statement of Jackson in his report on declining enrollment in Ontario (Connelly, Enns, & Jackson, 1979), who exhorted everyone not to lose sight of the fact that the child, as the learner, is the center of the school system and the only reason for its existence. Some may argue as to whether our students are our clients. But that question is not important at all. Simply put, student needs and aspirations must be main drivers of decision making in education.

I am by no means suggesting that we become servile, submissive, or subservient. After all, I discussed earlier the importance of assertiveness as a leadership competence. Nor am I suggesting that we accept the abuse that is sometimes leveled at those who work in public institutions. Professionalism certainly does not mean becoming sycophantic. But it does mean being thick skinned and constantly recognizing that we are in the business of service, and that people have the right to assess the quality of the service that we are providing and to provide us with feedback, which we must take seriously.

Reaching the heart of leadership means investing in people and building their capacity to become inveterate learners, truth seekers, and solution finders. It means rediscovering our mission, sharpening our resolve, and focusing on causes outside of ourselves. More important, it means addressing the needs of students and building the capacity of the people who attend to and support them.

Leadership Lessons Learned

1. Today, more than ever, leaders are being judged by the outcomes they achieve. A strong results orientation is now the expectation of parents and communities.

2. There is a renewed focus on accountability, with the continuing question of who is accountable for student achievements and other "results" expected in education. The debate rages on. Some feel that schools are responsible for student learning. Others argue that it has to be a shared responsibility between the home and the school.

3. The importance of teamwork cannot be overstated. In addition to the need for moving forward with a collective sense of mission and purpose, teamwork helps build future leadership capacity within an organization.

4. The primary motivation for leadership must be based on intrinsic motivation and must emanate from an internal locus of control. Leaders must not expect rewards or constant validation for their work.

5. Being attuned to the impact our leadership style and behaviors have on people and communities is essential learning for leaders. Every effort must be made to solicit feedback on these questions and, more important, to act on the recommendations.

6. It is essential to review our professional conduct guidelines and to reexamine what the expectations are for us as professionals and how we are meeting these expectations at different stages in our careers.

7. From time to time, we should reflect on the question of whether or not we are putting children first in all our actions and decisions, remembering that they are the center of the school system and the only reason for its existence.

8. As professionals, it is important for us to develop a thick skin and not get upset at what is perceived as negative feedback or what we may interpret as criticism about our work and our profession.

9. Educators provide a service. People have a right to criticize that service, and we have a responsibility to take the feedback seriously and to act on it in order to improve our practice.

10. Continuous professional learning must be at the heart of school and system improvement.

11. There is a common saying: "If you feed the teachers, they will not eat the children." We know that teachers are professionals and they will treat their children with professionalism. But this tongue-in-cheek statement is worth reflection if we are to pay attention to the professional, social, emotional, and other needs of our teachers and school leaders.

● ● ● ● ACTION STEPS FOR MAKING AN IMPACT

1. Utilize a variety of tools, methodologies, and feedback mechanisms to measure the impact of our work in order to determine what needs to be improved and what next steps should be in the improvement process.

2. Set clear targets with accompanying timelines and actions to realize specific and measurable achievements.

3. Engage in professional learning that has a strong basis in research. John Hattie's work in the area of Visible Learning, for example, should be an essential component of professional growth plans.

4. Use a variety of mechanisms and methodologies to gather information from students, staff, and community on the

(Continued)

(Continued)

quality of your leadership and the impact that we are having on the people and groups that you are serving.

5. Discuss with colleagues what constitutes competence and incompetence in your profession, in keeping with Albert Shanker's comments in this area, and use the criteria as guideposts for your assessment.

6. Determine concrete ways in which we can all enhance our professionalism by balancing professional autonomy with the cries for accountability that are reverberating in school districts across the globe.

7. Discuss with your staff and identify collaboratively the specific ways in which you will invest in your staff, build their capacity, and focus on their professional learning needs.

8. Develop (or revise) your school effectiveness and leadership framework to measure your effectiveness personally and collectively in delivering the services expected of your leadership.

9. Work with your business colleagues to examine quality frameworks and to see how educators and business leaders can find common ground on what constitutes leadership quality and accountability measures.

10. Build on what you have learned about what it takes to reach the heart of leadership in light of the key messages outlined in this book.

Conclusion: Reaching the Heart of Leadership—A Few Takeaways

The centrality of the role of leadership in successful organizations has been a major theme in this book. Coupled with the imperative to reach the heart, leaders who believe in continuous improvement are encouraged to develop leadership capacity in order to revitalize their schools and enliven their organizations. Stewardship—the ability to hold something in trust for a future generation—becomes essential. This certainly means a future generation of both leaders and the students they strive to influence.

Indeed, the needs of students has been addressed throughout this book. In fact, students have been placed at the center of all that we do. Addressing their needs represents the essence of our professionalism. I will therefore limit these concluding statements to the future of the adults and how we can redouble our efforts to reach the heart of leadership.

WHAT DO WE HOLD IN TRUST FOR FUTURE LEADERS?

The idea that leadership means leaving a legacy is also emphasized. That legacy includes a sense of urgency in getting things done, because, as I have argued, the children cannot wait.

Reaching the heart of leadership means getting in touch with what having power and influence means. If one believes in using power, in the traditional sense of the word, it must be "power with" or "power through" rather than a "power over" mentality. It means developing a high degree of self-knowledge and self-awareness, having high expectations for self and others, and having a passion for learning and achievement. It means adopting a holistic approach to education as we strive to educate hearts as well as minds. This includes a passion for the arts in the curriculum, for the role of character and citizenship education, for developing an entrepreneurial spirit, and for focusing on equity and inclusivity within our increasingly diverse contexts. It means becoming the strongest possible advocates for education that prepares graduates for global citizenship. It is our responsibility to ensure that we nurture graduates who think critically and analytically, who feel deeply and passionately, and who act wisely and ethically.

As I completed this book, I asked a few of my professional colleagues at different stages along the leadership spectrum for their ideas of what it means to reach the heart of leadership. Not surprisingly, some of their thoughts are remarkably similar to ideas discussed in this book. For example, a superintendent of schools in her first year of service said,

> Educational leaders reach the heart of leadership when their work is truly in service of students and families, particularly those less well served by education systems. When leaders works in concert with families and community to challenge the status quo, close achievement gaps, and change the trajectory of students so that they can reach

their full potential . . . then they do, indeed, reach the heart of leadership.

—Camille Logan
Superintendent of Schools
York Region District School Board

An expert in teaching, learning and curriculum review, development and implementation with whom I worked in Ontario, says:

Reaching the heart of leadership to me means working alongside teachers and leaders to do whatever it takes to improve the life chances of students—that is, ensuring reading, writing and thinking critically are possible for ALL.

—Dr. Lyn Sharratt
OISE, University of Toronto
International Consultant and Author

One of Ontario's leading curriculum leaders offered this insight:

Educational leaders should be agents of hope. They must believe in their hearts that they can make a positive difference in the lives of all children. Reaching the heart of leadership entails capitalizing on the unique opportunity leaders have to influence education, not only today but also tomorrow to ensure a better future for these students. This means building a blueprint for education systems that will achieve equity and excellence. It means that every decision is grounded in an unwavering commitment to ensure that every child succeeds. . . .

There are many qualities that educational leaders must possess in order to effectively lead, implement, and sustain change. They must have knowledge of policies, curriculum, budget issues, and other administrative processes, but that is not enough. They must lead with heart. Leading with heart means being able to empathize and relate to others. It means looking inward to personal values and beliefs to guide decisions and actions. Leading with heart means being an advocate for all students, but especially our most vulnerable students.

—Ruth Mattingley
Former Superintendent of Schools, and
Senior Executive Officer (Ret.)
The Literacy and Numeracy Secretariat

A director of education who has led one of the most successful school districts in Ontario in terms of student achievement, employee morale, and community engagement had this to say:

Leaders reach the heart of leadership when their actions continually speak louder than their words. Through consistency, perseverance, and fairness, true leaders show their passion and beliefs to those they work alongside and serve in their daily work. Reaching the heart of leadership becomes a reality when those they serve feel supported, empowered, and treated with respect and dignity, no matter the situation or challenges they encounter together. True leaders recognize and value the strength of others and continually seek to bring those strengths to the fore. Reaching the heart of leadership happens when, through their daily work, leaders truly inspire others to be the very best they can be, without prodding or exhortation.

—Larry Hope
Director of Education
Trillium Lakelands District School Board

And, finally, the perspective of one of Ontario's veteran educators— one who is credited for turning around his district, making it one of the most progressive districts in Ontario. For him,

A leader reaches the heart of leadership when there is the apprehension and acceptance of the state of mind and heart of another person or group. It is called empathy. Practically, the leader is able to put herself or himself into another person's reality. For the leader there is a deep underlying belief that everyone can grow and change and attain self- or group actualization. The heart spontaneously listens with responsiveness and acceptance, so that one is doing more than merely listening. One is seeking out ideas, experiences, and a synergy that makes a difference. Practically speaking, a major part of a leader's success must be how the people being led, and particularly young people, perceive and experience the world—how their attitudes and values demonstrate what it means to be a Canadian, and to take responsibility for the common good. To this end, how a leader changes attitudes and values is a large part of measured heart success.

At the core of universal success is student success. At the core of student success is the recognition that our young people must feel that their cultures and belief systems are accepted and included in their day-to-day learning. In these contexts, a leader must let all know that she or he is aware of systemic barriers and will do his or her best to remove them. When all is said and done, reaching the heart of leadership is a phenomenon that provides sensitivity to feelings and thoughts so that individuals and organizations can sense that there is also a heart inherent in leadership.

—Bill Hogarth
Director of Education (Ret.)
York Region District School Board

The perspectives of these successful educators all converge on the notion that a strong sense of service to students and parents, especially those in challenging circumstances, is essential—that leaders need to challenge the status quo, close achievement gaps, and be strong advocates for the children they serve. They need to be knowledgeable, demonstrate empathy, be aware of systemic barriers, and, more important, be willing to remove them. The leaders must practice what they preach, value their employees, facilitate their learning, bring out the best in them, change attitudes where necessary, and inspire them to do their best. They need to be agents of hope and optimism, strong in their determination to influence education generally, to achieve both equity and excellence, and, indeed, to make a difference. Leaders should simply lead with heart.

After almost four decades of experience at all levels of education systems, in rural and urban, public and private, Catholic and Protestant schools, I have learned many lessons along the way as I continue my professional quest to reach the heart of leadership. Here are a few of the lessons learned and the insights gained:

1. There must be a sense of urgency about improving schools. The children cannot wait.

2. Improvement goals must focus on what we want students to know, be like, and be able to do.

3. There can be no "throw-away" kids. Our society needs them all to be educated, productive, and self-sustaining citizens.

4. A strong focus on research-informed, high-impact strategies is essential. The focus has to be on what works.

5. It is necessary to adopt a holistic approach as we educate minds as well as hearts. While focusing on literacy, numeracy, and other subject areas, it is important to remember that character education and developing creativity, resilience, entrepreneurship, and other 21st century skills are also necessary.

6. Leaders must engage all partners, especially those who are expected to implement reforms. There must be a sense of ownership of the system priorities and directions.

7. Equity and excellence must go hand in hand. We must simultaneously raise the bar and close achievement gaps.

8. The purpose of improvement efforts is that they result in actions in the school and classroom, leading to improved student achievement and well-being.

9. The focus has to be on reaching the classroom. Learning must be visible. Results must be measurable.

10. Implementation matters. In organizations in which change initiatives fail, it is often because of inconsistent or superficial implementation.

11. Leaders must monitor implementation and student progress systematically. They must be prepared to make mid-course corrections to improvement plans as needed.

12. The essence of improvement is that school systems invest in people, build capacity, and focus on instructional effectiveness and leadership development.

13. Schools and systems that are focused on continuous improvement seek to learn from other countries and jurisdictions. Those that are most successful eschew competition, school ranking, privatization, and standardization.

14. Successful systems do not alienate or disparage their teachers and principals. Yes, they are demanding, but they treat their people with respect. They include them in decision making about instruction, school management, and leadership approaches, *inter alia*.

15. Successful organizations understand fully what motivates people.

16. Leaders who wish to lead from the heart always want to be sure that they have the right motives and intentions for the decisions that affect the lives of the people around them. They should ask themselves three questions:

    a. How will these decisions benefit students?

    b. How will the decisions benefit the community?

    c. How will the decisions benefit the society at large?

In sum, reaching the heart of leadership certainly requires self-knowledge, a constellation of interpersonal skills, and focused actions—many of which have been discussed in this book. It encourages educators to build on their current successes, keep their optimism alive, and continue the work that will take their districts to new heights of functioning and attainment.

References

Ahearn, K., Ferris, G., Hochwarter, W., Douglas, C., & Ammeter, A. (2004). Leader political skill and team performance. *Journal of Management, 30*(3), 309–327.

Allport, G. W. (1979). *The nature of prejudice*. Boston, MA: Addison-Wesley.

Alviridez, J., & Weinstein, R. (1999). Early teacher perceptions and later student academic achievement. *Journal of Educational Psychology, 91*(4), 731–746.

Anderson, S., & Kumari, R. (2009). Continuous improvement in schools: Understanding the practice. *International Journal of Educational Development, 29*(3), 281–292.

Begley, P. (2006). Self-knowledge, capacity and sensitivity: Prerequisites to authentic leadership by school principals. *Journal of Educational Administration, 44*(6), 570–589.

Brophy, J. (1983). Research on the self-fulfilling prophecy and teacher expectations. *Journal of Educational Psychology, 75*, 631–661.

Brophy, J., & Good, T. (1970). Teachers' communication of differential expectations for children's classroom performance: Some behavioral data. *Journal of Educational Psychology, 61*, 365–374.

Brown, M., & Trevino, L. (2006). Ethical leadership: A review and future directions. *The Leadership Quarterly, 17*(6), 595–616.

Brown, M., Trevino, L., & Harrison, D. (2005). Ethical leadership: A social learning perspective for construct development and testing. *Organizational Behavior and Human Decision Processes, 97*(2), 117–134.

Campbell, C., Fullan, M., & Glaze, A. (2006). *Unlocking potential for learning: Effective district-wide strategies to raise student achievement in literacy and numeracy*. Toronto, Canada: Ontario Ministry of Education.

Chism, M. (2016, January 2). Elevate your leadership in 2016. *The Huffington Post*. Retrieved January 1, 2017, from http://www.huffingtonpost.com/marlene-chism/elevate-your-leadership_b_8905052.html

Connelly, F. M., Enns, R. J., & Jackson, R. W. B. (1979). The Royal Commission on Declining School Enrolments in Ontario: A bulletin on the Commission and its studies in curriculum. *Journal of Curriculum Studies, 11*(1), 90–95.

Coombs, C. (2001). *Reflective practice: Developing reflective habits of mind* (Unpublished doctoral dissertation). University of Toronto, Canada.

Cooper, H., & Good, T. (1983). *Pygmalion grows up: Studies in the expectation communication process.* New York, NY: Longman.

Copeland, M. (2003). Leadership for inquiry: Building and sustaining capacity for school improvement. *Educational Evaluation and Policy Analysis, 25*(4), 375–396.

Datnow, A. (1998). *The gender politics of educational change.* London, England: Falmer Press.

de Boer, H., Bosker, R., & van der Werf, M. (2010). Sustainability of teacher expectation bias effects on long-term student performance. *Journal of Educational Psychology, 102*(1), 168–179.

Den Hartog, D. (2015). Ethical leadership. *Annual Review of Organizational Psychology and Behavior, 2*(1), 409–434.

Drucker, P. (1999). The new pluralism. In F. Hesselbein, M. Goldsmith, & I. Somerville (Eds.), *Leading beyond the walls: How high-performing organizations collaborate for shared success* (pp. 9–18). San Francisco, CA: Jossey-Bass.

DuFour, R., Eaker, R., & DuFour, R. (Eds.). (2005). *On common ground: The power of professional learning communities.* Bloomington, IN: National Education Service.

Ferris, G., Treadway, D., Kolodinsky, R., Hochwarter, W., Kacmar, C., Douglas, C., & Frink, D. (2005). Development and validation of the Political Skill Inventory. *Journal of Management, 31*(1), 126–152.

Flaum, J. (2010). *When it comes to business leadership, nice guys finish first.* Green Peak Partners. Retrieved from http://greenpeakpartners .com/resources/pdf/6%208%2010%20Executive%20study%20GP%20 commentary%20article_Final.pdf

Fraser, N. (2005). Reframing justice in a globalizing world. *New Left Review, 36*, 39–88.

Friedman, S. (2009, May 8). The most compelling leadership vision. *Harvard Business Review.* Retrieved from https://hbr.org/2009/05/the-most-compelling-leadership.html

Fullan, M. (1989). *What's worth fighting for in the principalship?* New York, NY: Teachers College Press.

Fullan, M. (2005). *Leadership & sustainability: Systems thinkers in action.* Thousand Oaks, CA: Corwin.

Fullan, M., Hill, P., & Crevola, C. (2006). *Breakthrough*. Thousand Oaks, CA: Corwin.

Gaskell, J., & Levin, B. (2012). *Making a difference in urban schools: Ideas, politics and pedagogy*. Toronto, Canada: University of Toronto Press.

Gini, A. (1998). Moral leadership and business ethics. In C. Ciulla (Ed.), *Ethics, the Heart of Leadership* (pp. 27–45). Westport, CT: Quorum Books.

Glass, R. (2007). What is democratic education? In W. Hare & J. Portelli (Eds.), *Key questions for educators* (pp. 83–86). Halifax, Canada: Edphil Books.

Glaze, A. (2011). Character development: Education at its best. *ASCD Journal: Reflections, 11*.

Glaze, A., Mattingley, R., & Andrews, R. (2013). *High school graduation: K–12 strategies that work*. Thousand Oaks, CA: Corwin.

Glaze, A., Mattingley, R., & Levin, B. R. (2012). *Breaking barriers: Excellence and equity for all*. Toronto: Pearson Canada.

Goleman, D. (2000, March/April). Leadership that gets results. *Harvard Business Review, 78*.

Goleman, D., Boyatzis, R., & McKee, A. (2002). *The new leaders: Transforming the art of leadership into the science of results*. London, England: Sphere.

Green, A., Preston, J., & Janmaat, J. (2006). *Education, equality and social cohesion*. New York, NY: Palgrave Macmillan.

Greenleaf, R. (1977). *Servant leadership: A journey into the nature of legitimate power and greatness*. Mahwah, NJ: Paulist Press.

Hassan, S., Mahsud, R., Yuki, G., & Prussia, G. (2013). Ethical and empowering leadership and leader effectiveness. *Journal of Managerial Psychology, 28*(2), 133–146.

Hattie, J. (2009). *Visible learning: A synthesis of over 800 meta-analyses relating to achievement*. New York, NY: Routledge.

Hawley, W., & Sykes, G. (2007). Continuous school improvement. In W. Hawley (Ed.), *The keys to effective schools: Educational reform as continuous improvement* (pp. 153–172). Thousand Oaks, CA: Corwin.

Helmrich, B. (2016). 33 ways to define leadership. *Business News Daily*. Retrieved January 1, 2017, from http://www.businessnewsdaily.com/3647-leadership-definition.html

Hoerr, T. R. (2017). *The formative five: Fostering grit, empathy, and other success skills every student needs*. Alexandria, VA: ASCD.

House, R., & Aditya, R. (1997). The social scientific study of leadership: Quo vadis? *Journal of Management, 23*, 409–474.

House, R., & Martin, P. (1998). Advocating for better futures for all students: A new vision for school counselors. *Education, 119*(2).

Jasper, K. (2014, January 12). Congeniality vs. collegiality: Cultivating communal culture in education [Blog post].

Jussim, L., & Harber, K. (2005). Teacher expectations and self-fulfilling prophesies: Known and unknowns, resolved and unresolved controversies. *Personality and Social Psychology Review, 9*(2), 131–155.

Kalshoven, K., & Boon, C. (2012). Ethical leadership, employee well-being, and helping: The moderating role of human resource management. *Journal of Personnel Psychology, 11*(1), 60–68.

Kalshoven, K., Den Hartog, D., & De Hoogh, A. (2011). Ethical leadership at work questionnaire (ELW): Development and validation of a multidimensional measure. *The Leadership Quarterly, 22*(1), 51–69.

Kendrick, M. (2008). Advocacy as social leadership. *The International Journal of Leadership in Public Services, 4*(3), 62–70.

Kovach, K. (1987). What motivates employees? Workers and supervisors give different answers. *Business Horizons, 30*(5), 58–65.

Kuklinski, M., & Weinstein, R. (2000). Classroom and grade level differences in the stability of teacher expectations and perceived differential treatment. *Learning Environments Research, 3*, 1–34.

Ladson-Billings, G. (2006). From the achievement gap to the education debt: Understanding achievement in U.S. schools. *Educational Researcher, 35*(7), 3–12.

Lammel, J. (2000). Principals and politics. *High School Magazine, 7*(6), 2.

Lloyd-Ellis, H. (2003). On the impacts of inequality on growth in the short and long run: A synthesis. *Canadian Public Policy, 29*(1).

Lugg, C. (2003). Sissies, faggots, lezzies, and dykes: Gender, sexual orientation, and a new politics of education. *Educational Administration Quarterly, 39*(1), 95–134.

Marx, G. (2014). *Twenty-one trends for the 21st century . . . out of the trenches . . . and into the future.* Bethesda, MD: Education Week Press/Editorial Projects in Education. Retrieved from www.edweek.org/go/21Trends

McCarthy, M., & Webb, L. (1990). Equity and excellence in educational leadership: A necessary nexus. In H. Prentice, H. Waxman, J. De Felix, & J. Anderson (Eds.), *Leadership, equity, and school effectiveness.* Thousand Oaks, CA: SAGE.

McGregor, D. (1960). *The human side of enterprise.* New York, NY: McGraw-Hill.

McKinsey & Company. (2009). *The economic impact of the achievement gap in America's schools.* Retrieved from http://mckinseyonsociety.com/downloads/reports/Education/achievement_gap_report.pdf

Mihelic, K., Lipicnik, B., & Tekavcic, M. (2010). Ethical leadership. *International Journal of Management and Information Systems, 14*(5), 31–41.

Miller, M. (2013). *The heart of leadership: Becoming a leader people want to follow*. San Francisco, CA: Berrett-Koehler Publishers.

Mintzberg, H. (1985). The organization as a political arena. *Journal of Management Studies, 22*(2), 133–154.

Neubert, M., Carlson, D., Kacmar, K., Roberts, J., & Chonko, L. (2009). The virtuous influence of ethical leadership behavior: Evidence from the field. *Journal of Business Ethics, 90*(2), 157–170.

NGA Center for Best Practices. (2002, May). The impact of arts education on workforce preparation. *Economic and Policy Studies (Issue Brief)*.

OECD. (2011). *Against all odds: Disadvantaged students who succeed in school*. Paris, France: Author.

Orenstein, P. (2002). Striking back: Sexual harassment at Weston. In S. Bailey (Ed.), *The Jossey-Bass reader on gender in education* (pp. 459–475). San Francisco, CA: Jossey-Bass.

Osberg, L. (1995, March). *The equity/efficiency trade-off in retrospect*. Paper presented at the Economic Growth and Income Equality Conference, Sudbury, Ontario, Canada.

Ouchi, W. G. (1981). *Theory Z: How American business can meet the Japanese challenge*. Reading, MA: Addison-Wesley.

Piccolo, R., Greenbaum, R., Den Hartog, D., & Folger, R. (2010). The relationship between ethical leadership and core job characteristics. *Journal of Organizational Behavior, 31*, 259–278.

Ratey, J. (2008). *Spark: The revolutionary new science of exercise and the brain*. New York, NY: Little, Brown and Company.

Realizing the promise of diversity: Ontario's equity and inclusive education strategy. (2009). Retrieved from www.edu.gov.on.ca/eng/policyfunding/equity.pdf

Reeves D. B. (2009). *Leading change in your school: How to conquer myths, build commitment, and get results*. Alexandria, VA: ASCD.

Reeves, D. B. (2016). *From leading to succeeding: The seven elements of effective leadership in education*. Bloomington, IN: Solution Tree Press.

Rosenthal, R., & Babad, E. (1985). Pygmalion in the gymnasium. *Educational Leadership, 43*(1), 36–39.

Roueche, J. E., Baker, G. A., & Rose, R. R. (1989). *Shared vision: Transformational leadership in American community colleges*. Washington, DC: Community College Press (a division of the American Association of Community Colleges).

Ryan, J. (2006). Inclusive leadership and social justice for schools. *Leadership and Policy in Schools, 5*(1), 3–17.

Sahlberg, P. (2011). *Finnish lessons: What can the world learn from educational change in Finland?* New York, NY: Teachers College Press.

Sandberg, S., & Scovell, N. (2013). *Lean in: Women, work, and the will to lead.* New York, NY: Alfred A. Knopf.

Schleicher, A., & Stewart, V. (2008, October). Expecting excellence: Learning from world-class schools. *Educational Leadership, 66*(2), 44–51.

Sergiovanni, T. J. (1990). *Value-added leadership: How to get extraordinary performance in schools.* New York, NY: Harcourt Brace Jovanovich.

Sergiovanni, T. (1992). *Moral leadership: Getting to the heart of school improvement.* San Francisco, CA: Jossey-Bass.

Shanker, A. (1985). The making of a profession. *American Educator: The Professional Journal of the American Federation of Teachers, 9*(3), 10–17, 46, 48.

Stein, N. (2002). Bullying as sexual harassment in elementary schools. In S. Bailey (Ed.), *The Jossey-Bass reader on gender education* (pp. 409–428). San Francisco, CA: Jossey-Bass.

St. George, A. (1983). Teacher expectations and perceptions of Polynesian and Pakeha pupils and the relationship to classroom behaviour and school achievement. *British Journal of Educational Psychology, 53*, 48–59.

Strike, K. (2007). *Ethical leadership in schools: Creating community in an environment of accountability.* Thousand Oaks, CA: Corwin.

Thiessen, D., & Anderson, S. (1999). *Getting into the habit of change in Ohio schools: The cross-case study of 12 transforming learning communities.* Columbus: Ohio Department of Education.

Tjan, A., Harrington, R., & Hsieh, T. (2012). *Heart, smarts, guts, and luck: What it takes to be an entrepreneur and build a great business.* Boston, MA: Harvard Business School Publishing.

Ulrich, D., Zenger, J., & Smallwood, N. (1999). Results-based leadership. *Executive Excellence, 16*(4), 13–14.

Walumbwa, F., Morrison, E., & Christensen, A. (2012). Ethical leadership and group in-role performance: The mediating roles of group conscientiousness and group voice. *The Leadership Quarterly, 23*(5), 953–986.

Weinstein, R. (2002). *Reaching higher: The power of expectations in schooling.* Cambridge, MA: Harvard University Press.

Wilhelm, W. (1996). Learning from past leaders. In F. Hesselbein, M. Goldsmith, & R. Beckhard (Eds.), *The leader of the future* (pp. 221–226). San Francisco, CA: Jossey-Bass.

Wilkinson, R., & Pickett, K. (2009). *The spirit level: Why greater equality makes societies stronger.* New York, NY: Bloomsbury Press.

Zhao, Y. (2012). *World class learners.* Thousand Oaks, CA: Corwin.

Zins, J., Bloodworth, M., Weissberg, R., & Walberg, H. (2007). The scientific base linking social and emotional learning to school success. *Journal of Educational and Psychological Consultation, 17*(2–3), 191–210.

FOR FURTHER READING AND REFLECTION

Bennis, W. G. (1989). *On becoming a leader*. Reading, MA: Addison-Wesley.

Block, Peter. (1993/1996). *Stewardship: Choosing service over self-interest*. San Francisco, CA: Berrett-Koehler Publishers.

Brice Heath, S., Soep, E., & Roach, A. (1998). Living the arts through language learning: A report on community-based youth organizations. *Americans for the Arts: Monographs, 2*(7).

Burns, J. M. (1978). *Leadership*. New York, NY: Harper & Row.

Datnow, A. (2002). Can we transplant educational reform and does it last? *Journal of Educational Change, 3*(3), 215–239.

Eisner, E. (2002). *The arts and the creation of mind*. New Haven, CT: Yale University Press.

Elghawaby, A. (2017, January 6). How false perceptions can hurt us all. *Globe and Mail*.

Fullan, M. (1982). *The meaning of educational change*. New York, NY: Teachers College Press.

Gardner, H. (1983). *Frames of mind: The theory of multiple intelligences*. New York, NY: Basic Books.

Guo, S. (2010). Toward recognitive justice: Emerging trends and challenges in transnational migration and lifelong learning. *International Journal of Lifelong Learning, 29*(2), 149–167.

Hadfield, C. (2013). *An astronaut's guide to life on Earth*. New York, NY: Little, Brown and Company.

Jensen, E. (2002, February). Teach the arts for reasons beyond the research. *The Education Digest*.

Kennedy, K. (1974). *Career preparation: Suggestion for teachers*. Lexington: Kentucky Curriculum Development Center, University of Kentucky.

Leithwood, K., Mascall, B., Strauss, T., Sacks, R., Memon, N., & Yashkina, A. (2006). Distributing leadership to make schools smarter. *Leadership and Policy, 6*(1), 37–67.

London, M. (2008). Leadership and advocacy: Dual roles for corporate social responsibility and social entrepreneurship. *Organizational Dynamics, 37*(4), 313–326.

Manasse, A. L. (1986). Vision and leadership: Paying attention to intention. *Peabody Journal of Education, 63*(1), 150–173.

Maxwell, J. (2011). Leadership ladder. *Success*. Retrieved from http://www.success.com/article/john-maxwell-leadership-lad

Murphy, J., & Hallinger, P. (1993). *Restructuring schooling: Learning from ongoing efforts*. Thousand Oaks, CA: Corwin.

Noguera, P. (2006). A critical response to Michael Fullan's "The future of educational change: System thinkers in action." *Journal of Educational Change, 7*(3), 129–132.

Ohler, J. (2000, October). Art becomes the fourth R. *Educational Leadership*.

Osborn, R., Hunt, J., & Jauch, L. (2002). Toward a contextual theory of leadership. *The Leadership Quarterly, 13*(6), 797–837.

Peddie, R. (2015, December 14). The importance of having a vision. *Globe and Mail*.

Index

CØRWIN LEADERSHIP

Leadership that Makes an Impact

Charlotte Danielson
Harness the power of informal professional conversation and invite teachers to boost achievement.

Liz Wiseman, Lois Allen, & Elise Foster
Use leadership to bring out the best in others—liberating staff to excel and doubling your team's effectiveness.

Eric Sheninger
Use digital resources to create a new school culture, increase engagement, and facilitate real-time PD.

Russell J. Quaglia, Michael J. Corso, & Lisa L. Lande
Listen to your school's voice to see how you can increase engagement, involvement, and academic motivation.

Michael Fullan, Joanne Quinn, & Joanne McEachen
Learn the right drivers to mobilize complex, coherent, whole-system change and transform learning for all students.